*To: Mother Mildred*
*The draught season is over,*
*Your Harvest Time is Now!—*
*Prepared us for God Predestined Blessings. Thank*
*you for being such a source of blessings and*
*a dear Mother to Shannon & I! Love*
*Bishop Harrison*

# The Judah Apostolic
# & Prophetic Chronicles

## Volume One

*"And the Word Of The Lord Came*
*Unto Me Saying"*......

Here A Little....
There A Little....!

Then All At Once!

## APOSTLE ROSS D. GARRISON, JR.

Mildred Johnson
281 Bantry Dr.
Vacaville, CA 95688

D1684909

The Judah Apostolic & Prophetic Chronicles, Vol.1
© Copyright 2010 Apostle Ross D. Garrison, Jr.

ISBN 978-1-4507-1889-9

**Bishop Saylike Productions - Publishing Company**
Email address: saylikepubco@aol.com
Telephone 1-888- (9Saylik) 927-9545

Book Cover Design by
Alicia Finley, Signature WebSites &
Graphic Design Company

Typeset and book design by
Per-Fect Words Publishing Company
www.per-fectwords.com

# Table of Contents

*Personal Dedication*
*Acknowledgement*
*Personal Endorsements*

*In Honor Of My Beloved Parents*
The late Rev. Dr. Ross Douglas Garrison, Sr., &
Mrs. Verdie Lee Dokes-Garrison

# About The Author

*"You will carry the Gospel of Jesus Christ to the World"* *Prophetic* Words spoken over his life by his father, the late Rev. Dr. R.D. Garrison Sr. over 47 years ago. The tenth child, born to the late Rev. Dr. R.D. and Mrs. Verdie L. Garrison Sr. Apostle Dr. Ross D. Garrison is currently celebrating forty four years in the Gospel Music Industry an accomplished pianist and organist. In August 1996 he was consecrated to the office of Bishop by the late Bishop William H. Bryant Jr. In 2003 he was confirmed as an Apostle of the Lord Jesus Christ by Apostle R. L. Vinson. In 2006 he received two Honorary Doctorates of Divinity one from St. Thomas Christian College in Jacksonville Florida Dr. Zamekio T. Jackson President and a Doctorate as well as a diploma from the Bell Grove Theological Seminary Dr. AC Ambers and Marie B. Bailey President. He has spent thirty one years Preaching and Teaching and twenty eight years as The Set Man of Judah the Gathering Place Inc. Oakland, CA, along with his wife, Pastor Shannon D. Garrison.

Blessed, anointed, and gifted by God, Apostle Garrison serves not only as the Set Man, but also in the capacity as the Lead Minstrel in Praise & Worship, with the blended grace of the Apostolic and Prophetic flowing together, with hands raised, hearts lifted and the souls of the masses bowed down in worship its an experience waiting to happen.

The Songs of the Lord is all too familiar within the House of Judah. This grace anointed gift have blessed the masses with simplicity in just striking a chord and hearing the voices respond in the high praises to God. This sets and creates an atmosphere for the miraculous to happen and appear.

A Gift to the Body of Christ, he has preached extensively throughout the United States and internationally, having ministered in Australia, China, Thailand, Bangkok and Burma. A well sought conference/crusade/revivalist speaker. Apostle RD Garrison hosts the Annual Judah Int'l Gathering (held in July – see website www.judahgathering.org) where people have gathered as far as from Australia, Hong Kong, China, South Africa, to the Oakland/ San Francisco Bay Area for the past 24 years to his credit. An Apostolic and Prophetic Voice called to the Nations! God's Mouthpiece in these last days endeavoring to usher men and women to their destined call in God, fulfilling the prophetic word spoken over his life!

Apostle Garrison has been a benefit and great asset to the community. His humble spirit allows him to be approached by people from all walks of life. The burning desire to fulfill the call on his life to preach the gospel to the poor, heal the brokenhearted, set captives free, give sight to the blind, set at liberty those who are bruised and preach the acceptable year of the Lord compels him to continue to press toward the mark of the higher calling in Christ. The Judah Apostolic and Prophetic Chronicle Vol.1 is just the beginning of many more to come. I trust that this book has and will minister life in the midst of your dry barren places, and bring forth in you the fountain of living waters and fresh oil from the Presence of the LORD.

†RD Garrison Jr. – Apostle

# Foreword

We live in a time when words flow in abundance, but wisdom seems to come in short supply. We pack more on our calendars, but seem to miss opportunities more and more. We have become so accustomed to living in our own strength that we have missed the value one gains through quiet reflection and steady growth.

In this incredible book from Apostle R.D. Garrison, you will discover a key necessary for understanding the mind of God for you and your destiny. God does nothing outside of process. There is an order in everything that God does. If you comprehend God's reason, you begin to understand HIS nature.

God moves in seasons. He operates in moments of the miraculous that were actually years in the making. Someone prayed, someone gave, someone suffered as a good soldier, something happened piece by piece to lead us to this divine suddenly. Nothing just happens!

In the rush and roar of life, we forget to sit before Him and gain wisdom. So, God in His divine kindness to His creation sends a voice of experience wrapped in a cloak of prophecy to declare to us that God is actually teaching us a lesson if we would only step back to see it. Apostle Garrison is a man sent to the Kingdom for such a time as this.

He has proven himself to be a man of prayer and prophecy, a man of decrees and dimensions, and a man of the Word and of worship and a man with an ear to hear what the Spirit is saying to the churches. Don't miss the valuable opportunity you are presented with as you explore these pages.

*Prophet Michael Dalton*

# *Introduction*

Chronicle: an ordered record; a detailed report; record or narrative. Chronicle; is an account of historical events presented in the order in which the events took place; like a timeline the term has it's origin in the Greek word for time "chronos."

The author of a chronicle is known as a chronicler, chroniclers often record events they witness themselves during their own lifetime. (Webster's New International Dictionary)

The Judah Apostolic & Prophetic Chronicles - "And the Word of the Lord Came Unto me Saying" Vol. 1 are writings derived from my personal daily devotional time spent in the presence of the Lord through early morning prayer, praise, and worship.

Every true worshipper can witness to the fact that the Number One key to having and maintaining a fresh anointing is seeking and staying in the presence of the Lord Jesus and loving God with all of your heart (Psalms 27:8). Number Two: living a daily life of: repentance, being transparent and decreeing & declaring the Word of Faith over my life, family and ministry every day. Number Three: seeing the need of accountability upon one's self. King David declared in Psalms 103:1.

Bless the Lord, O my soul: and all that is within me bless his holy name. "Bow down and worship before the throne, decreeing and declaring, Grace, Grace."

The sub-title of the book "Here A Little, There A Little, Then All At Once" was taken from many Apostolic & Prophetic words that I ministered at Judah which inspired the name Judah Chronicles.

Nothing in the timing or economy of God comes all at once. I personally believe God designed it that way. We need time, patience, space and grace to grow into what God has promised. Many of you like me have been a part of many Presbytery meetings where the servants of the Lord (Apostles and Prophets) have spoken great, mighty and powerful things that we should do. Now it's been sometime between what was spoken and what has manifested.

Today's time isn't any different from the way it was in the Old and New Testaments. There is a "Time Effect" that all of us must embrace before there is a manifestation of the spoken word. Abraham walked faithfully and endured until the appointed time. King David did not ascend to the throne right away as a matter of fact after his Presbytery was over he went back to doing what he did prior to being called to the anointing of sacrifice.

It is my desire to share with the world how magnificent, marvelous and mighty Gods word can be when applied to our everyday lives. It would be selfish to hold on to this word and not share it with everyone willing to read it, believe it, and apply it. So please enjoy and my prayer is that it becomes a reality for the world and blesses the world with the same magnitude that it blessed me.

*Chapter 1*

# How It All Began
# Judah Apostolic
# Prophetic Chronicles

O ver the past two years I began sending out a series of bi-weekly emails to my congregation entitled, "The Judah Apostolic & Prophetic Chronicles…And the Word of the LORD came unto me, saying…" The Chronicles are the result of my personal prayer and intercession time with the Lord. Prayer is the life line and breeding ground to everything in God. The late Rev. Dr. C.J. Anderson use to say, "Prayer is the key to heaven and faith unlocks the door". My Dad and Mom were mighty prayer warriors. As a child growing up and into my adulthood, I have fond memories of watching them pray all the time. Seeing this caused me to desire a consistent prayer life as well. After reading and studying the Gospels I also desired to have a prayer life like the Lord Jesus " in the morning rising up a great while before day he went out and departed into a solitary place, and there He prayed." (Mark 1:35) Jesus prayed more than he preached or taught. This speaks volumes to me! As a result of much discipline, I now have a consistent time of when and where I pray, I must say that this has definitely paid off and this book is a result of that.

My mind goes back to the very first time I felt the Hand of the LORD literally touch me and I thought that it was one of my parents checking on me in the middle of the night. I had no idea of the particular or specific "Calling" of the LORD at that time upon my life, and Him calling me to prayer. It wasn't until after I accepted Christ into my life as my LORD and my Savior at a Youth Retreat the fourth Sunday in May, 1979 that I realized it was the Lord. The following first Sunday in June my father, the late Rev. Dr. R.D. Garrison, Sr. and a visiting Minister Elder Williams, A

Lieutenant General in the United States Army laid hands on me and the LORD baptized and filled me with the Gift of the Holy Ghost and Fire at the tender age of (16) during our Holy Communion Service. This was the beginning of my journey process of "Here A Little."

I acknowledged and accepted my life's calling into the Ministry. I would fast, read for knowledge and pray for an understanding and the LORD through the Holy Spirit began to reveal His voice to me through the study of His Word, which developed and stirred up that hunger and thirst for righteousness (obedience to trust and to take God at his word). This brought and taught me to know, hear, listen, understand and hearken to the voice of the LORD in a greater and more intimate way. I began to pray, LORD give me an ear to hear by the Spirit. This was preparing me for the next dimension of the anointing and ministry, "There A Little" The Pastoral Calling (August 15, 1982).

I can remember The Spirit of the LORD awakening me out of my sleep countless times speaking, talking and revealing people's names, their faces and showing me times and seasons of the present and the future without any human knowledge and those things have come to pass. I have seen and witnessed the faithfulness of the Lord to His Word and Servants and not one word has fallen to the ground (1 Samuel 3:19). I truly bless His Name for enabling and trusting me with the affairs of His people and seeing the Kingdom of God advance.

My spiritual heritage has given me a well-rounded perception, understanding and knowledge of the grace gift and the Mantle of the Apostolic and Prophetic Anointing that God has placed upon my life. Our families' spiritual inheritance is a combination of the following denominations: Christian Methodist Episcopal, Baptist, Church of God In Christ and The Sanctified Holiness Church. All of which have greatly influenced my life and made me the Man of God that I am. I am fully aware that as a servant of the Lord I have a mandate to impart, raise up and usher many other men and women of God to identify and embrace their God ordained purpose and destiny with holy boldness.

Through prayer and intercession (in the fourth watch of the night between 3AM & 6AM) God has given me so many countless visitations and revelation knowledge of His word for my life, my family, our church and now the world. If there is one thing I know, I know the voice of the Lord and you can know that same voice too. All it takes is discipline and obedience. Move at His every command and watch him do exactly what He said He would do. The past 31 years of my teaching and preaching ministry and the last 28 years of my life serving as The Set Man over the House of Judah, I can share with you from experience that whatever you purpose in your heart God will grant you your heart's desire (Psalms 37:4). Having His presence in my life, has kept me on a fresh cutting edge of knowing the very heart beat of God and being an instrument in His hands to be used as He sees fit. A voice called to the nations to bring forth glad tidings of great joy, have been my lifelong dream and is now a reality…"Then All At Once!"

I pray that your life will be blessed, enriched and strengthened as you read through the Judah Apostolic and Prophetic Chronicles birthed through my time spent with the Lord Jesus and the Holy Spirit through PRAYER!

Your obedience will be someone else's deliverance, salvation, breakthrough, hour of restoration and confirmation. Vol.1 of The

Judah Apostolic & Prophetic Chronicles, this is just the beginning, many more volumes are to follow so stay tuned!

I pray and speak blessings of "Here A Little, There A Little, and then get ready for the All At Once Blessings!"

*Chapter 2*

# Faith Moving Foward

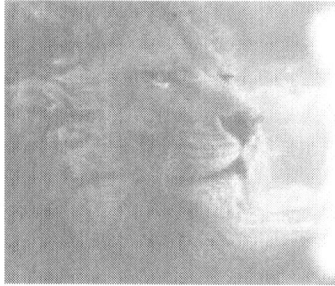

—————————————— ■ ——————————————

It is impossible to move forward while looking backwards. To advance forward requires one to pay attention, focus, to take heed and follow direct directions. To have faith, is to have a hearing ear, "So then faith cometh by hearing, and hearing by the word of God." (Romans 10:17) KJV.

At the close of 2009, the LORD commissioned me to do three things in 2010 in regards to the Word of the LORD and the vision for the House of Judah…

---

**1) Teach My People Faith**

**2) Move Them Forward**

**3) Engage My People in Becoming Commanders of the Wealth Covenant.**

---

There is a strong sense and witness within my Spirit that God is shaking up some things in the heavenlies, Isaiah 43:18, 19 "Behold I will do a new thing." As we moved out of the single digits of the 21$^{st}$ Century with the completion of the year of 2009, the ending of one era, the number nine indicating total completion, fullness of time and the expected time a mother is to carry her unborn to term. The New Year 2010 is the dawning of a new era. Many things are being finalized, which will set the stage for new beginnings, opportunities and new doors being opened while other doors are being closed.

We need to develop a greater sense of discerning the difference between a loss and the process of elimination. There is a difference, a loss is something of value that we once had, enjoyed and were very fond of. While the process of elimination is that which was never meant to be and nothing for you, I, or anyone else to waste any tears over, there's no need to cry over spilt milk. The process of elimination helps you to see, what your next options are. There is no need to get or become stuck! Get up, get over it, and move on!

As 2009 was coming to a close which represented the end and finalizing of the single digit era and the beginning of the double digit era of the 21$^{st}$ Century, I could not help but to think and to compare, the little knowledge that I have of knowing how to finalize a CD and DVD once it is finished recording. These words appear in bold letters **"TO FINALIZE PRESS OK."** The instruction manual suggests that while the recorder is going through this finalizing process, that you **"DON'T TOUCH ANYTHING."** You could potentially damage what has been recorded and captured!

What we don't see happening is that the recording is sealing what has been captured, which will enable you to go back and listen and preview. For the mere fact that you are alive in 2010, there are some things that God has already **FINALIZED, SEALED**, and **GUARANTEED** that is going to happen for you in this season.

We have entered into the double digest era. I encourage every believer to set your hope in God and anticipate that **"2010"** is your year to receive **DOUBLE! DOUBLE!** (1 Samuel 1:5) states that Elkanah gave Hannah a **"WORTHY PORTION"** which is equivalent to a **"DOUBLE PORTION BLESSING."** Read (**Isaiah 61:7**) "For your shame ye shall have **DOUBLE**; and for confusion they shall rejoice in their portion: therefore in their land they shall possess the DOUBLE: everlasting joy shall be unto them." Prophetically we decree, declare and say that this year **"2010"** is symbolic to Joseph's second son **"EPHRAIM,** whose name means, **"DOUBLE FRUITFUL."** Yes, God himself shall cause you and I to be fruitful in the land of our afflictions, which will automatically enable us to **"Manasseh"**, forget the hardship of not only our father's house, but also the last nine years! We need to mix faith within ourselves and believe God and become familiar with the supernatural. To those of us who serve as **"RULING ELDERS"** in the Lord's Church, the Apostle Paul admonished the saints (**1 Tim. 5:17**) "Let the elders that rule be counted worthy of **DOUBLE HONOR."**

There are many things that are about to unfold, many things that are about to be unmasked. The treasures of darkness and hidden riches that have been hid, covered up and gone unaware, are about to be discovered (Isaiah 45:1-3) KJV. There are some things that are purposed and set a side for a specific time to manifest. I believe that this year 2010, is the designated time and season for these things to be.

There are some people, places and things that you have seen for the very last time. Hear me by the Spirit of God; while it may not be every thing at once, some things are just simply over! It's time to move forward, reevaluate, reorganize and get ready to relocate. Moving forward requires and demands that you have a changed mindset. Get ready to do some things differently. As a matter of fact, get ready to step outside the boat and jump into the water. God is ready for you to step out into the outer limits, take those limits off of Him, your self, your faith, the anointing and step back and watch God go to work on your behalf. Moses had received instructions from the LORD God Jehovah concerning moving Israel forward and relocating them to the Land of Canaan. They could not see it because of their slave mentality.

(**Exodus 14:12, 13**) "[Is] not this the word that we did tell thee in Egypt, saying, Let us alone, that we may serve the Egyptians? For [it had been] better for us to serve the Egyptians, than to die in the wilderness. (**Verse 13**) "And Moses said unto the people, Fear not, stand still, and see the salvation of the LORD, which he will shew to you today: for the Egyptians whom ye have seen to day, ye shall see them again no more for ever."

Notice the word of the LORD, there are some things being finalized right now. Some things that you have experienced, gone through, had to put up with, some were favorable while others where unfavorable, but God says, **"You will see them again no more for ever."**

The Word of the Lord to Moses was why are you crying to me, "Speak to the Children of Israel and tell them I said, GO FORWARD." I'm not sure who is reading this book and this particular page, but I take full use of the authority of God upon my life and speak to you and your destiny that has been on hold and I say to you by the power and authority of the Holy Spirit, MOVE OUT NOW IN JESUS NAME!

2010, is the dawning of a new era of awesome new beginnings. Great and wonderful expectations are just waiting on the horizon for the people of God. But there is something that you are required to do. In the book of (Philippians Chapter 3:13, 14) Apostle began to admonish the saints at Philippi, with some explicit instructions:

> Phil 3:13  Brethren, I count not myself to have apprehended: but [this] one thing [I do], forgetting those things which are behind, and reaching forth unto those things which are before.

> Phil 3:14  I press toward the mark for the prize of the high calling of God in Christ Jesus.

There are a lot of things I could do, but he narrows it down to "This one thing I do…Forgetting those things which are behind" I don't mean any harm, but we might need to have a clinic moment right here... When you step into a persons' sensitive zone they have a tendency to fold their arms, which is an indication that their guard is up and they have shut down on you, because you are requiring accountability.

Forgetting hurts, monumental pain, confronting individuals, having to relive and rehash all of those unsettled issues and sentimental emotions, it is not an easy human thing to do but it is possible. The course of healing a wounded spirit is not clinically, or naturally cured by administering drugs. There is only one true source for the spirit and soul to be healed, and my friend; I take great pleasure by offering and introducing Jesus Christ, God's only begotten Son. For every automobile that Toyota, GM. Chrysler, Mercedes, and Rolls Royce have made, when parts began to break down and repair is needed, you take it back to the manufacturer and let them repair what is broken. "The spirit of a man will sustain his infirmity; but a wounded spirit who can bear? (Proverbs 18:14) KJV.

We have held on to so many old hurts from our childhood that it has now carried over into our adulthood and we are no more the better. The Apostle Paul said, we ought to "forget those things which are behind, and reach forth (FORWARD) to those things which are before." Engage yourself into the press and begin to move forward. You're not hurting or hindering anyone but yourself. It's not worth it, forgive and forget. Don't play the cat and mouse game by pushing unresolved issues under the carpet, or walking out the door, you want to make certain that every door is properly closed and shut tight. Take my word for it, as a Pastor, I have sat at my desk the past twenty-eight years of my life praying, talking and advising countless of thousands of people, on how to resolve unsettled issues, how to close doors properly, and move on with their lives.

A song comes on the radio, a piece of paper falls that triggers your memory lapse and it starts all over again. Your subconscious will automatically go way back and retrieve those feelings and emotions, which start the cycle back up.

It's time to press towards the mark for the prize of the high calling of God in Christ Jesus. 2010 is a clear indication that you can't stay parked where you have been. Your mind set has got to change. Your value systems have got to change. Your hope has got to change. Your expectation has got to change.

What is one of the greatest challenges in Moving Forward? The fact of leaving what is all too familiar and going where you have never been is challenging. Don't be afraid for your feet to touch the ground. When Moses brought Israel out of Egypt, they went on dry ground. No water, nowhere in sight. Had there been any water left in their attempt to cross over, they would have walked in mud and brought the evidence of where they had been over into their future.

In the Book of Joshua, chapter 3 – Joshua, arose and removed Israel from Shittim (the place of the wood tree or forestry or preparation). This is the site and location where the acacia trees, where they cut the wood for the furnishings of the Tabernacle which was overlaid with gold. As they began to approach Jordan, they were there three days before they crossed over. Jordan speaks of dying or death to ones self. Jordan is viewed as the place where you offer yourself, your will, your mind, your soul and your body up to the LORD.

Joshua commanded the officer to speak to the children of Israel these instructions, when you see the Ark of the Covenant of the LORD your God and the priest the Levites bearing, then ye shall remove from your tent and go after it. So many people in the Body of Christ have missed God, failing to associate the Priest and the Levites in conjunction with God, His Presence and Anointing. They are inseparable (Joshua 3:3, 4). When you see the Leadership starting to move, then you move. Note, that it wasn't just the Priest and the Levites moving, it was what they were moving (The Presence). We need leaders in this 21st Century that are just not mobile, but they are carrying an anointing, which makes them movers and shakers.

## Are You Ready to Go Where you've Never Been?

Every new venture requires a setting apart from one thing, so you might be set apart unto something else. Verse #4b "For you have not passed this way heretofore" There is a sense in my knowing that great exploits are waiting to happen, when the feet of the Priest touch the waters. Verse #13 – Jordan dried up. Can you sense and feel that something is about happen?

Let me give you a clue and share with you some insightful revelation knowledge that the Holy Spirit revealed to me. What would you say if I told you that God made Joshua a very wealthy, influential and well prosperous man. God made Joshua very rich through his FEET! His possession was not by his confession alone; his feet played a major role in the obtaining and securing of his wealth, riches and fortune.

Joshua 1:3 Every place that the sole of your foot shall tread upon, that have I given unto you, as I said unto Moses.

<u>2Cr 5:7</u>  (For we walk by faith, not by sight

<u>John 5:5</u>  And a certain man was there, which had an infirmity thirty and eight years.

<u>John 5:6</u>  When Jesus saw him lie, and knew that he had been now a long time [in that case], he saith unto him, Wilt thou be made whole?

<u>John 5:7</u>  The impotent man answered him, Sir; I have no man, when the water is troubled, to put me into the pool: but while I am coming, another steppeth down before me.

<u>John 5:8</u>  Jesus saith unto him, Rise, take up thy bed, and walk.

<u>John 5:9</u>  And immediately the man was made whole, and took up his bed, and walked: and on the same day was the Sabbath.

Now do you see and understand, that the way into your wealthy place of possessions and accessing the promises of God, is not by your confession only, but it's also done by you and I taking and making the initiative your possession by the sole of foot.

How far are you willing to walk, to get what God says belong to you? Joshua and children of Israel walked marched around the City of Jericho once for 6 days without saying anything. Then on the seventh day, they walked marched 7 times, Joshua gave the charge and commanded the people to shout – "Shabach" and the walls fell down flat. The same thing is about to happen for you. (Joshua 6)

Supernatural Doors are being opened and there is an open door for you. What do you do when a door is open? You begin to walk through them. There are all kinds of doors that God has finalized to be open to you. Some doors, you pull, while other you push. Some doors slides open automatically as a result of a sensor mechanism. Then there is the rotating door, that just goes around and you walk in and then walk out. There is power in the sole of your feet. God made a promise to Joshua, that every place where the sole of his foot shall tread, that have I given unto you, as I said unto Moses. The places where you walk in 2010, God is going to give you total access into green pastures. "Let them shout for joy, and be glad that favor my righteous cause: yea let them continually say, Let the LORD be magnified, which hath pleasure in the prosperity of his servants (Psalm 35:27)."

Now look in the book of Isaiah 61:7 "But ye shall be name the priest of the LORD: men shall call the ministers of our God: ye shall eat the riches of the Gentiles, and in their glory shall you boast yourselves." Verse #7 – "For your shame ye shall have double; and for confusion they shall rejoice in their portion: therefore in their land they shall possess the double: everlasting joy shall be unto them."

In this year of 2010, we have stepped over into an entirely new era of double digits. God is ready to show you off to the world, by causing you to experience double Fruitfulness. God has written the name Ephraim over your life. Expect to receive Double Honor, A Double Portion, more than what you can handle, count, or even see. Get ready to launch out into the deep and let down your nets for the drought. You have entered into your season of the Overflow. This is Gods' set time of favor upon your life, your family, your health, your wealth, your business. Every witty invention is going to enable you to become a commander of the covenant wealth.

This is your time and season to arise and shine, for your light is come and the GLORY of the LORD is raised upon you! Your territory has been enlarged. Expect everything in your life to become progressively better!

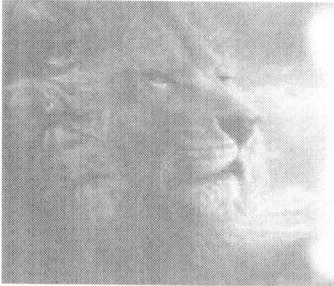

*Chapter 3*

# Here A Little...
# There A Little...
# And Then
# All At Once!

**Mildred Johnson**
281 Bantry Dr.
Vacaville, CA 95688

———————————▪———————————

In my journey process as a believer, disciple and Servant of the Lord, I have discovered in my personal study and research of the scriptures that there is a method and pattern that God through the Holy Spirit relates and reveals His plans, purpose and will to His people. In the book of (Isaiah 46:10) God through the age of time has always declared the end from the beginning. From ancient times God has proclaimed the things that are not yet done, saying "My counsel shall stand and I will do all my pleasure."

Therefore, we are encouraged and led to believe that our lives literally starts from the end working it's way to the beginning. While we are walking from the beginning to the end, we're trying to figure out and understand this step-by-step faith walk and process. From the days of Adam to the 21st Century, God has never revealed or showed any man or woman His total plan and will for their lives. The process and method in every generation has always been, "Here A Little, There A Little, Then All At Once." That is the aftermath in which we have finally come through a series of events, the process of elimination and then we arrive at the point of "The Blessings of the Lord which maketh rich and He addeth no sorrow to it!

As we continue to walk by faith, we come to know the perfect plan, will, and purpose as to why the Lord brought us the way He did to teach us total dependence on Him. Once the word goes forth out of Gods mouth it shall not return to Him void, but it shall accomplish that which He pleases, it shall prosper in the thing where He sent it (Isaiah 55:11). Every word that God has spoken was established, complete, done and settled, at that very moment. It is like a contractor building a house or a sky scrapper. You have the blue print in hand but what you are looking at is to be done in stages over a period of time.

It doesn't matter at what time the sky scrapper is completed. The blue print is symbolic of what prophesy is, "history written in advance." This is exactly the definition of what I am speaking and sharing with you in this chapter and the title of this book. What God has spoken, declared and decreed over your life, you may not see in living color all at once but as you continue to look back at the blueprint every now and then, you will get a glimpse, here a little, there a little, and then all at once!

> Isaiah 28:10   For precept [must be] upon precept, precept upon precept; line upon line, line upon line; here a little, [and] there a little:

> Isaiah 28:13   But the word of the LORD was unto them precept upon precept, precept upon precept; line upon line, line upon line; here a little, [and] there a little;

## One might ask, what is the meaning of a precept?

Command, ordinance, oracle, a commandment, an authoritative rule for action; in the Scriptures generally a divine injunction in which man's obligation is set forth ("a guide to instruct and give instructions.")

If God was to show, tell, or reveal to you or I every major and minor detail, let the record reflect we wouldn't be able to comprehend, discern, digest, let alone maintain a level head and still walk by faith. I will at this point side with those from old school, "God is to wise to make a mistake, and put more on you than you can bear."

The wisest man King Solomon wrote that "It is the glory of God to conceal a thing: but the honor of kings is to search out a matter." (Proverbs 25:2). We need to take the time to search out and discover the "Method to God's Mystery." Many people focus on reaching their destiny, while they miss the valuable lessons from and through their journey process. Over the years in reading the Bible all the way through from cover to cover Genesis to Revelation, you always see, glean and get something different every time you read it.

One day while studying and working on the chapter entitled "Amar – "The Power of your Words and the things that you Say" this thought came to me, "Here A Little, There A Little, and Then All At Once." My inner being (my Spirit) was moved and overwhelmed. I knew at that very instant, that there was more to these simple words. I had no idea at the time that this would be the title of my very First Book Project. To God be the Glory, Honor, and Praise!!!

When I look into the scriptures, I constantly see various scenarios that give me faith, hope and encouragement to trust and believe God, no matter how impossible things may appear up close or from a far distance. The title of this book reflects so many wonderful passages of scripture and biblical characters whose life reality speaks right into our current circumstances and where we live today. For instance when we read the life story of Abram (at age 75) and Sarai (65) they receive a word from God to depart from their country, kindred, and from his father's house, unto a land that God will show and reveal to them in time. Note that what God had spoken did not come to pass the very next day, week, month, or the following year.

We read Gods decrees and declaration to Abram in the book of Genesis:

> Genesis 12:2 And I will make of thee a great nation, and I will bless thee, and make thy name great; and thou shalt be a blessing:

> Genesis 12:3 And I will bless them that bless thee, and curse him that curseth thee: and in thee shall all families of the earth be blessed.

> Genesis 12:4 So Abram departed, as the LORD had spoken unto him; and Lot went with him: and Abram [was] seventy and five years old when he departed out of Haran.

The Word of the LORD always sets and establishes the foundation for what God is about to do. Amos 3:7 states the following, "Surely the Lord GOD will do nothing, but he revealeth his secret unto his servants the prophets."

Although God revealed the end of the matter to Abram of what His plan and intent was at this point, this was just the beginning of what would be carried out over the next "25 YEARS" of his life. Take note, Abram nor Sarai did not have a clue that what God had spoken would not happen all at once, but they would later come to realize it would be staged, here a little and there a little. No one is exempt from the process of the Word of the LORD being tried. We all have to prepare ourselves to walk through some valley experiences and speak to the mountains and command them to be removed, while walking this thing out called Faith! 2 Corinthians 5:7.

This is a word of warning to the wise, have you noticed in your life, that there is always that one faithful person, that no matter what the LORD said or says, they are the faithful to find a loop hole, and try to make you believe contrary to what God has just spoken to build up your faith to receive, to hope and to expect. Somehow Sarai, found a way into Abrams ear to convince him, that regardless to what God said in (Genesis 15) about her bearing Abram a son, no doubt in reading (Genesis 16) they had been trying with no success, remember what I just said, "beware how things may appear up close or in a far distance" it could be deception working at its best. You are just that close to "Something Is About To Happen!"

Sarai convinces her husband Abram to go in unto her handmaid Hagar and it may be…that I may obtain children by her." The bible says that Abram hearkened to the voice of Sarai. The word "hearken" is different than listening. Hearken is defined:" to listen with the intent of doing what is spoken or suggested." Now we all know that this was an accident waiting to happen. But in spite of his sin of disobedience, which is now a distraction, detour and will eventually produce a delay, thank God not a denial…"The Word of the LORD still Stands" (Hallelujah Jesus!).

Now like Daddy and Momma use to teach and tell us growing up as young children, sometimes listening to the wrong advice, will cost you dearly. Thank God for grace and mercy, and the blood of Jesus which enables Him to look beyond our faults every time and see our needs. He is obligated to see us through to glorification. Somehow He's the only one that can unscramble our eggs and yet serve us some sunny side up eggs with great delight. God is always faithful to fulfill His Word all by Himself (Hebrews 6:13 -20).

Weariness has a way of finding its way into the lives of those who do well. (Galatians 6:9) we are encouraged that we shall reap if we faint not.

> Genesis 17:1 And when Abram was ninety years old and nine, the LORD appeared to Abram, and said unto him, I

[am] the Almighty God; walk before me, and be thou perfect.

Genesis 17:2 And I will make my covenant between me and thee, and will multiply thee exceedingly.

Genesis 17:3 And Abram fell on his face: and God talked with him, saying,

Genesis 17:4 As for me, behold, my covenant [is] with thee, and thou shalt be a father of many nations.

Genesis 17:5 Neither shall thy name any more be called Abram, but thy name shall be Abraham; for a father of many nations have I made thee.

Genesis 17:6 And I will make thee exceeding fruitful, and I will make nations of thee, and kings shall come out of thee.

Genesis 17:7 And I will establish my covenant between me and thee and thy seed after thee in their generations for an everlasting covenant, to be a God unto thee, and to thy seed after thee.

Genesis 17:8 And I will give unto thee, and to thy seed after thee, the land wherein thou art a stranger, all the land of Canaan, for an everlasting possession; and I will be their God
Genesis 17:9 And God said unto Abraham, Thou shalt keep my covenant therefore, thou, and thy seed after thee in their generations.

Genesis 17:10 This [is] my covenant, which ye shall keep, between me and you and thy seed after thee; Every man child among you shall be circumcised.

Genesis 17:11 And ye shall circumcise the flesh of your foreskin; and it shall be a token of the covenant betwixt me and you.

We see that there is a name changed for both Abram to Abraham and Sarai to Sarah. I was always taught and instructed that whenever you see a name change in biblical writings, it speaks to a change in nature, character, personality and attributes. Now Abraham receives a command from the LORD who appeared to him as the Almighty God (**EL SHADDAI, THE MANY BREASTED ONE, THE GOD WHO IS MORE THAN ENOUGH**).

This is the message he heard, **"walk before me and be thou perfect."** This word **perfect** "tä·mçm'" is defined: (**complete, whole, entire, sound, healthful, unimpaired, innocent, having integrity, what is complete or entirely in accord with truth and facts**). It is now 24 years later from the time they left and departed from Haran until now. Still there is no sign of the promise child yet.

Keep this factor in mind, "God is obligated to see you through to glorification." This is what God does, He reassures and revisits the promise that He made 24 years earlier. Can you see the picture becoming even clearer now than it was before? God works in stages, just as the contractor builds according to what he sees on the blue print. Although the blue print and photo reveals what the final and finish product will reflect, it is still a work in progress. Here A Little There A Little Then All At Once!

I speak prophetically into your spirit, life and whatever current circumstances and situation that is staring you right in the face now, ***"God is about to make You Laugh*!"** Laughter is a sign of joy, rejoicing, gladness and pleasurable surprise. The title of this book is prophetic in nature. It gives you the ability to interpret the divine will of God for your life, the past, current and future seasons of your life. There is divine definition given in this simple but most profound word. I want to encourage you to stand firm in this fact that what hasn't happened for you yet, it's about to happen for you NOW! Yes, you need to know and I am glad to tell you as you read this book, that "Your Waiting Period Is Over Says The LORD"!

Look at what the scriptures says in Genesis 17:16,17; 18:9-15...And get ready to LOL...."LAUGH- OUT – LOUD"...in the face of all that looks and have the appearance of hopelessness, worthlessness, that which seems impossible, especially if your back is up against the wall and you can't and don't see a way out..LOL...Watch what God is about to Do...!!!

> Gen 17:16 And I will bless her, and give thee a son also of her: yea, I will bless her, and she shall be [a mother] of nations; kings of people shall be of her.

> Gen 17:17 Then Abraham fell upon his face, and laughed, and said in his heart, Shall [a child] be born unto him that is an hundred years old? and shall Sarah, that is ninety years old, bear?

> Gen 18:9 And they said unto him, Where [is] Sarah thy wife? And he said, Behold, in the tent.

> Gen 18:10 And he said, I will certainly return unto thee according to the time of life; and, lo, Sarah thy wife shall have a son. And Sarah heard [it] in the tent door, which [was] behind him

> Gen 18:11 Now Abraham and Sarah [were] old [and] well stricken in age; [and] it ceased to be with Sarah after the manner of women.

> Gen 18:12 Therefore Sarah laughed within herself, saying, After I am waxed old shall I have pleasure, my lord being old also?

> Gen 18:13 And the LORD said unto Abraham, Wherefore

did Sarah laugh, saying, Shall I of a surety bear a child, which am old

Gen 18:14   Is any thing too hard for the LORD? At the time appointed I will return unto thee, according to the time of life, and Sarah shall have a son.

Gen 18:15   Then Sarah denied, saying, I laughed not; for she was afraid. And he said, Nay; but thou didst laugh.

Abraham the Father of Faith and his wife Sarah; who were old, well stricken in age; and it ceased to be with Sarah after the manner of women (Genesis 18:11) Now if this was baseball, you know the rules, 3 strikes and you're out! Absolutely no questions asked. That's the rule. But God made an exception to the rule, (Thank You Jesus) Here is the reason why 1Peter 5:10. But the God of all grace, who hath called us unto his eternal glory by Christ Jesus, after that ye have suffered a while, make you perfect, establish, strengthen, settle [you]. Abraham and Sarah finally arrived at the place called, "Then All At Once." This is where God is about to bring you. Are you ready for the over flow? A 3:20 anointing is being released upon you now. Yes, that's Ephesians 3:20 Now unto him that is able to do exceeding abundantly above all that we ask or think, according to the power that worketh in us! Get ready to prosper, expect the supernatural power of God to show up in your life and stand back and watch God work in and on your behalf...

Now look back at where they came from. God promised, declared, and decreed in (Genesis 12:1-4) "And I will make of thee (Abram) a great nation, and I will bless thee and make thy name great, and thou (Abram) shall be a blessing: verse 3. And I will bless them that bless thee: and curse him that curseth thee: and in thee shall all families of the earth be blessed."

Now do the math, between chapters 12 and chapter 17 there is a huge gap and a timeline lapse of 24 years. Wow, can you imagine what that felt like and the images that went along with that kind of patience, waiting on the LORD and being of good courage? God had to strengthen his heart to wait that long...hmmm?

What do you do when God has made you a promise and that promise has not come to pass? Can you imagine the different thoughts, feelings, and emotions that are running in his mind? God did I miss you? Have I missed my day of visitation? Are you still holding sin and sins against me?

Because God is the Grand Conductor, He knows how to pull every part and piece together of our broke, torn and shattered life, and produce a symphony of praise and worship to His ears and His heart from what seems and appears to us as Bad! Bad! Bad news! If anybody can, I know that God can do anything but FAIL!

When we look back at the beginning timeline in Genesis 12, Abram was 75 and Sarai 65 ten years younger. Looking at numerology the number 75 speaks of separation and coming to the end of oneself. There were some other changes that had too and needed to take place in order for what was and had been spoken to come to pass at the appointed time. I am inclined to believe, that God wittedly waited until they were old, stricken in age, and it was well past Sarah's ability to bear children. Why Garrison? So they could not claim any glory, or honor to themselves for reproducing after their kind.

In Paul's letter to the Romans chapter 4:17-25 <u>Romans 4:17</u> (As it is written, I have made thee a father of many nations,) before him whom he believed, [even] God, who quickeneth the dead and calleth those things which be not as though they were.

Romans 4:18  Who against hope believed in hope, that he might become the father of many nations, according to that which was spoken, So shall thy seed be.

Romans 4:19  And being not weak in faith, he considered not his own body now dead, when he was about an hundred years old, neither yet the deadness of Sara's womb:

Romans 4:20  He staggered not at the promise of God through unbelief; but was strong in faith, giving glory to God;

Romans 4:21  And being fully persuaded that, what he had promised, he was able also to perform

Romans 4:22  And therefore it was imputed to him for righteousness.

Romans 4:23  Now it was not written for his sake alone, that it was imputed to him;

Romans 4:24  But for us also, to whom it shall be imputed, if we believe on him that raised up Jesus our Lord from the dead;

Romans 4:25  Who was delivered for our offences, and was raised again for our justification.

Now after twenty-five years, the ending report is this, the Apostle Paul, concludes where Moses left off, by giving us a reason for putting our hope and our trust in the true and living God. Whatever God has spoken and promised He is well able to perform it and bring it to pass. Paul's writing is clear and to the point, in verses (17-25) God calleth those things which be not as though they were. Now you would think, after what we would call the big mess up, why even try. Verse 18, "Who against hope believed in hope, excuse me right here, but I feel a shout coming on (Hallelujah). Regardless of the fact that he laid with Hagar and produced Ishmael, Abraham was still looking, hoping and expecting Sarah to experience morning sickness.

Yes, she went from barrenness to fruitfulness, from being nonproductive to productive.

> <u>Hebrews 11:11</u> Through faith also Sara herself received strength to conceive seed, and was delivered of a child when she was past age, because she judged him faithful who had promised.

No matter how long your promise from God may take, rise up and receive strength for yourself, trust and believe God. Count and judge him faithful. For one thing is for certain, God is not a man, that He should lie; neither the son of man, that He should repent: hath He not said it and shall He not do it? Or hath he spoken, and shall he not make it good? (Numbers 23:19)

The final conclusion is this, Abraham refused to stagger (to become intoxicated with unbelief) he was strong in faith, doing something, "Giving God the Glory." Whatever you are facing right now, stop, and lift your hands, open your mouth and salute His Majesty through a word of Praise, Thanksgiving, Honor, Adoration, and Admiration out of a grateful Heart!

God finally made Sarah, Hannah, and Elizabeth along with so many countless other barren to produce. Expect manifestation to show up in your life soon!

You see the secret to Here A Little, There A Little, Then All At Once is biblically based. It requires one to become acquainted with God and learn to develop a relationship with Him. The Prophet Hosea put it like this, "Then shall we know, [if] we follow on to know the LORD: his going forth is prepared as the morning; and he shall come unto us as the rain, as the latter [and] former rain unto the earth." (Hosea 6:3)

It may not happen as you think or thought it should, but rest assure, the promises of God are sure and always on time. Even when you think that God is late. Look back over your life and expect it to happen anyway. How? Here A Little, There A Little, and you know what.....THEN ALL AT ONCE!

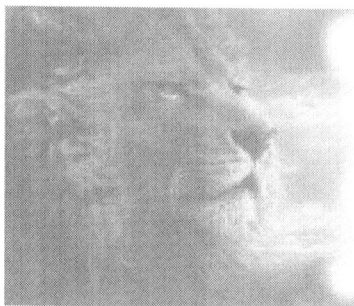

*Chapter 4*

# The Power Of Your Amar

Have you ever wondered what the most creative force in the world is? Could it be our nation's military army, parliamentary government, or the vote of a particular party? Well, when you stop to think about it, it all boils down to one thing. When you run out of answers and resources, the final analysts are the power and the authority of the words that we speak, use and say every day of our lives. Good, bad, ugly and indifferent.

Are you aware of the power of your tongue? Very few people have given this much thought, let alone the attention that it deserves. The epistle of James talks about "the tongue" and categorize it as the smallest member of the human anatomy. Here's what the scriptures teaches about the tongue:

> James 3:5 Even so the tongue is a little member, and boasteth great things. Behold, how great a matter a little fire kindleth!

> James 3:6 And the tongue [is] a fire, a world of iniquity: so is the tongue among our members, that it defileth the whole body, and setteth on fire the course of nature; and it is set on fire of hell.

I trust that this will peak your interest and you will begin right now at this very moment, to make a conscience decision about the choice words that you use from this point forward.

It is important as children of the "Most High God" that we follow in his likeness in order to experience Kingdom blessings, benefits and prosperity. God has provided his people with the ability to see what they say through the power of their confession or "Amar." Many believers fail to confess their faith to move past the familiar toward a destiny filled with the wealth of the Kingdom.

The power of "Amar" was demonstrated by God himself when he spoke "let there be light" and there was light in the presence of darkness filled with confusion, disorder and misery (Gen. 1:1-3). The earth was without form and void and darkness was on the face of the deep. I find it personally interesting how an awesome God is attracted to any state of confusion to bring order where there is chaos through the simple form of speaking one word. Imagine, in the midst of all of this confusion the spirit of God always hovers and moves where negativity appears to be the ruling principality.

One word from God will change any situation! Many believers both past and present continue to exercise their God given right and ability to declare and decree words of faith, hope and great possibilities of turning negative situations (i.e. environments) into possible realities. We are admonished to declare and decree change into our atmosphere.

The word of the Lord came to me concerning the power of the words we speak which is our "Amar." The Holy Spirit revealed to me that the Lord not only wanted me to change my "Amar", he also wanted to transform my thinking Proverbs 23:7 states, "As he thinketh in his heart so is he."

The thoughts we think and the words we speak, they both produce and create ....

The word of the Lord provoked me to seek the meaning of "Amar" and its multifaceted purposes. I think it is noteworthy to mention that the word "Amar" appears in the Old Testament 5,280 times.

"Amar" means:

(1) To say, to speak, to utter; to tell to declare...

(2) To name, to mention...

(3) To designate...

(4) To answer...

(5) To call...

(6) To admonish; to promise...

(7) To praise, to say in the heart, to think...

(8) To intend, to purpose...

(9) To expect, to boast, to act proudly...

God changed the discourse of the world's condition by pronouncing to the prevailing darkness and confusion that existed within the universe. By uttering, "Let there be light" He created a living force designed not only to illuminate the natural Earth but to introduce His people to the revelation knowledge of His kingdom, spiritual insight, wisdom and understanding of the creative essence of "Amar."

Biblical examples like Jesus and John the Baptist were agents of change who altered circumstances by simply declaring the word of the Lord through faith. By connecting their faith to the word they preached, they were able to dominate the demonic powers through their declarations. Their "Amar" coupled with the anointing and faith allowed them to speak change into the atmosphere, hemisphere, stratosphere and ionic-sphere (which affected the climate and environment of their day). Paul said "Repent, turn, make an about face go in the opposite direction which you were headed" For the Kingdom of heaven is at hand." Crooked places were made straight, rough places were made smooth, regional jurisdictions were transformed and the lives of the people were totally changed as a result of the word preached mixed with faith in them that heard it.

## A Basic Bible Kingdom Principle

Rom 10:8  But what saith it? The word is nigh thee, [even] in thy mouth, and in thy heart: that is, the word of faith, which we preach; (the zamar is in your mouth and heart). But it must be spoken!

Rom 10:9  That if thou shalt confess ( agree) with thy mouth the Lord Jesus, and shalt believe in thine heart that God hath raised him from the dead, thou shalt be saved.

Note what the Prophet Isaiah had to say about the power of a people's "Zamar" Say/Speech, the word of their mouth"…You have the power to move heaven and earth

Isaiah 42:22 "But this [is] a people robbed and spoiled; [they are] all of them snared in holes, and they are hid in prison houses: they are for a prey, and none delivereth; for a spoil, and none saith, Restore"

Proverbs 6:2 Thou art snared with the words of thy mouth, thou art taken with the words of thy mouth.

Job 22:28 Thou shalt also decree a thing, and it shall be established unto thee: and the light shall shine upon thy ways.

2 Corinthians. 4:13 We having the same spirit of faith, according as it is written, I believed, and therefore have I spoken; we also believe, and therefore speak;

Mark 11:24 Therefore I say unto you, What things soever ye desire, when ye pray, believe that ye receive [them], and ye shall have [them].

## The Power of God's Spoken Word In Creation

<u>Gen 1:3</u>  And God said, Let there be light: and there was light.

<u>Gen 1:6</u> And God said, Let there be a firmament in the midst of the waters

<u>Gen 1:8</u>  And God called the firmament Heaven. And the evening and the morning were the second day

<u>Gen 1:9</u> And God said, Let the waters under the heaven be gathered together unto one place

<u>Gen 1:10</u>  And God called the dry [land] Earth

<u>Gen 1:11</u>  And God said, Let the earth bring forth grass, the herb yielding seed,

<u>Gen 1:14</u> And God said, Let there be lights in the firmament of the heaven to divide the day from the night

<u>Gen 1:20</u> And God said, Let the waters bring forth abundantly the moving creature that hath life

<u>Gen 1:20</u> And God said, Let the waters bring forth abundantly the moving creature that hath life

<u>Gen 1:26</u> And God said, Let us make man in our image, after our likeness: and let them have dominion over the fish of the sea, and over the fowl of the air, and over the cattle, and over all the earth, and over every creeping thing that creepeth upon the earth

<u>Gen 1:29</u> And God said, Behold, I have given you every herb bearing seed, which [is] upon the face of all the earth, and every tree, in the which [is] the fruit of a tree yielding seed; to you it shall be for meat

> <u>Gen 1:31</u>   And God saw every thing that he had made, and, behold, [it was] very good

There is a creative power and force to be reckoned with in making biblical faith declarations and daily decrees over your life, your family, finances, your health, home, property, destiny and everything that God has called you forth to do in Jesus Name.

## Are You Ready To ZAMAR Something?

Let's start right here and now:

Restore! Lord Save me! Deliver me! Lead me! Guide me! Being broke and suffering from lack is nowhere in sight for me, my family, my finances, health, wealth, or my church ministry! LORD, Send Now Prosperity! Wealth and riches are in my House! Give us this day our Daily Bread! God is blessing me so well everybody thinks that I am doing something illegal! Who said that you had to pay for it anyway! Samson decreed and declared these words to the Lord God Jehovah, Help me! Strengthen Me! One more Time! The Word will work for you, when you begin to work the Word!

As you begin to practice and exercise the power and authority of your Zamar, (your speech, spoken words out of your mouth) you will begin to see and experience people, places, and things set in motion, ready to be restored back into your life and their proper origin. The word is nigh thee, even in your mouth and in your heart, the Word of Faith that we speak!

Something is about to happen. Restoration is coming into every area of our life, spirit, mind, body, soul, ministries, family, finances, health, etc. etc. etc. Say it, name it, declare it, and decree it, and it shall come to pass! (Don't hate or hesitate, just participate!!!)

Set the atmosphere with your ZAMAR from the Word of the LORD and you will See what you Say!

*Chapter 5*

# I Will Give You Rain In Due Season

———————————————■———————————————

I want to dedicate this chapter to all those who have felt like giving up and throwing in the towel. Some of you are facing serious difficult times and seasons. You are wondering "God where are you? Where have you been?" I also want to encourage every Front Line Soldier who has been assigned and designated with and without a title, credentials or degrees of honor. I don't have to know you personally to share this message and word that I received from the Lord. Since I'm not sure into whose hands this book will fall, let me share this secret with you. Your life is about to experience some radical changes that you have been waiting for to come to pass. I want to speak prophetically into your life and to tell you that, it is not by chance or accident that this book was published for you, because God had you on His mind. How do I know this? Because you're reading the right book, at the right time, on the right page!

I have some good news to tell you. Regardless of who you are, where you come from and where you are about to go. If you are a child, teenager, or the CEO of a Fortune 500 Company, I have an urgent message to share with you. You need to know that the reason why you are reading this chapter at this very moment is because **"Your Drought Season Is Over!"**

Trust me when I tell you, that if you thought for one moment that your life was over and done, you couldn't be more wrong or off. If this book is not for anyone else, I know that it is for you. It is my practice and belief that nothing in life just happens without there being a purpose. As a Born Again Believer, disciple and

Apostle I know and believe that God still talks and speaks to His servants in the Twenty-Fitrst Century as He did in the First Century Church and too the patriarchs of old. Do you believe that God still moves in mysterious ways and His wonders are to be performed? Then you should know that the God of the Bible still talks and speaks as He spoke to Abraham, Isaac, and Jacob.

One morning, the Lord awakened me out of my sleep speaking these words to me *"I will give you rain in due season."* Can you imagine, waking up out of a deep sleep to the voice of God speaking and rehearsing these words over and over in your spirit and ears. Envision with me right now that those dry, dead, non productive seasons in your life are now OVER. Every area, every arena of your life that lacked moisture, God says, "I have given you rain in your due season! It's time to have a party and celebrate the dawning of your new beginnings. Get ready to experience the long awaited Harvest you have been waiting for."

The Rain is here! You need to be well assured that no matter what it looks like, feels like, or what it's been like, something good, positive and exciting is about to happen for you. I don't know what you need right now. Maybe it's a miracle or the restoration of a relationship that has gone bad. Let me encourage you to expect the unexpected. Although your harvest has been delayed, it is not denied. A major breakthrough is coming into your life. Yes, I want you to know that whatever it is you need to manifest "It's About to Happen!"

I want to share these three scriptures with you that the LORD revealed to me pertaining to rain in due season.

> Lev. 26:4 Then I will give you rain in due season, and the land shall yield her increase, and the trees of the field shall yield their fruit.

> Deut. 11:14 That I will give [you] the rain of your land in his due season, the first rain and the latter rain, that thou mayest gather in thy corn, and thy wine, and thine oil, cattle, and in the fruit of thy ground, in the land which the LORD sware unto thy fathers to give thee.

> Deut. 28:12 The LORD shall open unto thee his good treasure, the heaven to give and remain inve the rain unto thy land in his season, and to bless all the work of thine hand: and thou shalt lend unto many nations, and thou shalt not borrow.

Because the Lord is giving us rain in due season, we need to be in a posture to receive all He has for us. The LORD caused me to know and to understand that in the face of adversity we must take hold to faith, courage, and praise. We cannot become weary in well doing, why you may ask? Because this is our DUE SEASON, IF WE FAINT NOT! A few weeks ago, the Lord spoke this passage of scripture to me Psalm. 27:13 "I would have fainted unless I had believed to see the goodness of the Lord, in the land of the living."

The tribe of Judah (The Praise & Worship crowd) God's universal mighty warriors, you and I have been called to show forth (demonstrate) the praises of the LORD from the rising of the sun to the going down of the same. We have to hold on to the promises of God like never before. In the face of being challenged and what appears to be difficult, you can draw strength from Ephesians 6:16 "Above all, taking the shield of faith, wherewith ye shall be able to quench all the fiery darts of the wicked." (1 Peter 2:9, 10)

> 2Cr 4:13 "We having the same spirit of faith", according as it is written, I believed, and therefore have I spoken; we also believe, and therefore speak.

We are not going through anything differently than those from the Old and New Testament era. We have the same spirit of FAITH. Same test, same trials, same tribulations, same devil, same demons and most of all Jesus Christ, the same, yesterday, today, and forever! This is Spiritual Warfare that we are facing...Take on a Kingdom Strategy and let take it by force! (Matthew 11:12)

> 2Cr 10:3 For though we walk in the flesh, we do not war after the flesh: 2Cr 10:4 (For the weapons of our warfare [are] not carnal, but mighty through God to the pulling down of strong holds;)

> 2Cr 10:5 Casting down imaginations, and every high thing that exalteth itself against the knowledge of God, and bringing into captivity every thought to the obedience of Christ;

> 2Cr 10:6 And having in a readiness to revenge all disobedience, when your obedience is fulfilled.

## Posture Your Faith To Receive Manifestations From The Word of The Lord!

Faith cometh by hearing and hearing by the Word of God! Incorporate the fore mentioned scriptures into your daily confession, decrees and declarations. He that hath an ear let him hear what the Spirit saith to the church! God has never left His people without a witness. The Lord moved and impressed upon me to share and to give you His Word. Therefore, I encourage you with this, "Let the Word Do the Work." Paul preached to the church at Corinth, that their Faith would stand in the power of God, and not in man's wisdom or philosophy/theory! I give you the Word of God...Read it! Believe it! And obey it! God has given me Rain in Due Season! (Romans 10:17; Hebrews 11:11). The Rain is not coming, The Rain is here and it's now. This is Your Due Season. We have heard it said before; we have been hearing it for a while; now hear it again! Stand back and watch God bring every promise to pass.

*Hear the Word of the Lord....*

"I WILL GIVE YOU RAIN IN DUE SEASON"....THIS IS OUR MOMENT DESIGNATED...GET READY TO FLOURISH, BLOOM, AND BLOSSOM LIKE YOU HAVE NEVER BEFORE! RAIN in the scriptures speaks of several types and shadows...the focus and symbolism here in the use of this word is "Refreshing, Revival, Renewal, and Restoration." THESE ARE TIMES OF REFRESHING THAT COME FROM THE PRESENCE OF THE LORD!

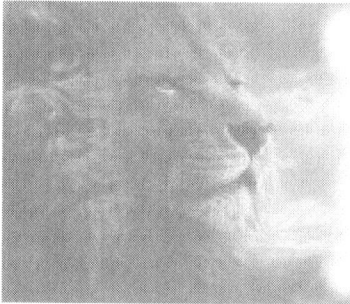

*Chapter 6*

# Pause For The Cause

————————■————————

I bid you Godspeed, the comfort of the Holy Spirit, His guidance and directions which always leads to victory!

Have you ever had one of those moments where you just stop dead in your tracks, you just pause for a moment to ponder, think, consider and rethink through a choice or decision that really needs to be re-evaluated? Well, this is that chapter.

I simply just want to share a word of encouragement with you. I'm not sure where you are, or even perhaps what you are going through, or what might be facing you at this very minute. I recommend that as soon as you can, read one of my all time favorite passages of scripture from the Old Testament found in Psalms 46:10 "Be still, and know that I [am] God: I will be exalted among the heathen, I will be exalted in the earth."

Whenever I hit a low point and find myself in Lodebar (the place of low pasture) this is my rescue scripture without fail. It lifts me up and strengthens my faith and courage time after time again. It admonishes us to "Be still (silent, motionless) and know that I am God." Our relationship with Christ is the binding factor that enables us to weather the storms of life, help us maneuver our way through every tight and uncomfortable places, wherever pressure is being applied.

Life has a way of throwing us so many curve balls at once, that many times we really don't know what direction to look? Have you ever felt like you were being hit on every side and all you needed was just a moment to gather your composure so you would know how to strategize. Don't feel bad you are not alone. Somehow things have a way of turning around and working in your favor.

The Apostle Paul in his letter to the Corinthians sent them these words which ministered grace, hope, and comfort to their souls:

> 2Cr 4:7 But we have this treasure in earthen vessels, that the Excellency of the power may be of God, and not of us.
>
> 2Cr 4:8 [We arc] troubled on every side, yet not distressed; [we are] perplexed, but not in despair;
>
> 2Cr 4:9 Persecuted, but not forsaken; cast down, but not destroyed;
>
> 2Cr 4:10 Always bearing about in the body the dying of the Lord Jesus, that the life also of Jesus might be made manifest in our body.

God has done such a work of grace in our lives many times we don't even realize the value and the powerful effects of the Holy Spirit's presence in our lives. God allows us to go through various experiences to show and prove to us this valuable treasure we have in earthen vessels. This transcended immeasurable unlimited grace with the surpassing greatness of his power is actively working within us demonstrating the excellency of His power.

Wow, to think that this great God of the universe is living on the inside of us by faith it is through grace! He is destroying the works of the devil and enabling you and I to live victoriously through Christ Jesus our LORD. "Greater is He that is within us than he that is in the world." Thank God that we possess the victory that overcomes the world, even our faith, all because of Christ's victorious resurrection.

We need to "Pause for the Cause" and recognize that without these temporary inconveniences, what would God have to show off within and upon us? No matter how we look at the process, it's a win, win, situation. Although we are troubled on every side (Yes), yet not distressed (No) we are perplexed (Yes), but not in despair (Right), persecuted (Yes), but not forsaken (Right) cast down (Yes) but not destroy (Absolutely). Now all of this may not look right or even sound right, yet the Word of the Lord keeps coming to remind us over and over again that we have the victory. In times like these, what do you do? Well, there's really only one thing to do, "Count it all joy, when you fall into divers temptations. Knowing this the trying of your faith worketh patience." You can come out and through with the ability to last.

> Exd 1:11  Therefore they did set over them taskmasters to afflict them with their burdens. And they built for Pharaoh's treasure cities, Pithom and Raamses.

> Exd 1:12  But the more they afflicted them, the more they multiplied and grew. And they were grieved because of the children of Israel.

Now you would think that this would and should leave a bad taste in their mouth. But look back at the text, what they experienced as a result was increase, prosperity and promotion you become stronger, wiser and better! Through every test and trial God is fortifying, building and strengthening our character. The process of engagement enables us with the ability to withstand the wiles, scheme's, tricks and tactics of the devil. We are girded, armed and dangerous. Yes, our revelation knowledge of who Christ is enables us to endure the gates of Hell which cannot prevail against us.

There is no way possible that we are going to escape having to face some challenging moments, (which are spiritual growing pains). God's method and process of bringing us into full maturity is never the way we think or assume. Therefore, we always rely on His wisdom and dare not lean to our own understanding. But trust in the Lord with all of your heart; and he shall direct your paths.

> 2Cr 4:17 For our light affliction which is but for a moment, worketh for us a far more exceeding [and] eternal weight of glory;

Notice the Apostle's tone, tenor, and posture here: "Light affliction." Have faith in God, and know that if it is a light affliction, then He knew that you would be able to bear and get through it! Another favorite passage of scripture is:

> 1 Peter 5:10
> "But the God of all grace, who hath called us unto his eternal glory by Christ Jesus, after that ye have suffered a while, make you perfect, stablish, strengthen, settle [you].

No matter where you are in the process, it won't last long; pause, breathe, and keep moving. Here's the reason why; God is obligated to see you through, to glorification. You will come out and come through, more than a conquer with flying colors. Believe to see the goodness of the Lord in the land of the living...May the Lord God bless you real good!

*Chapter 7*

# Sound Effects

S ound is defined as traveling vibrations through air, water, or some other medium, especially those within the range of frequencies that can be perceived by the human ear. At sea level and freezing point, the speed of sound is 1,220 kilometers/760 minutes per hour. Something that can be heard!

## PSALMS 47:1, 2,5; 100:1-4; ACTS 16:25

Psa 47:1 [To the chief Musician, A Psalm for the sons of Korah.] O clap your hands, all ye people; shout unto God with the voice of triumph.

Psa 47:2 For the LORD most high [is] terrible; [he is] a great King over all the earth.

Psa 47:3 He shall subdue the people under us, and the nations under our feet
.

Psa 47:4 He shall choose our inheritance for us, the excellency of Jacob whom he loved. Selah

Psa 47:5 God is gone up with a shout, the LORD with the sound of a trumpet.

Psa 89:15 Blessed [is] the people that know the joyful sound: they shall walk, O LORD, in the light of thy countenance.

Psa 107:2 Let the redeemed of the LORD say [so], whom he hath redeemed from the hand of the enemy;

## Implication of Sound

The implication of sound is an impression of somebody or something formed from limited but significant information, especially information lately received.

### Ear Shot

Ear shot refers to the distance or area within which something can be heard.

### Effects

Effects are results, outcomes and successes that bring about a change in the atmosphere, climate, environment in something or somebody. The ability to achieve change occurring as a direct result of actions.

From the very moment of conception, out of sight and out of mind, the **sound effect** of a distant faint heart beat that could only be heard by him who neither sleeps nor slumbers. God himself surely indicates the first sign of life begun in outer darkness.

Although, unaware by the mother and the clueless father to be, his seed fertilized her egg and now impregnated and attached itself to the walls of her womb. The process of regeneration and a new birth is on the way. Time and science has perfected it's practice over time. We now have the capability in the very early stages of hearing the "Sound Effects of a baby's heart beat" through the means of an (ultra sound and we can now see the image and features in 3-D of our unborn child via sonogram).

Uniquely designed, hand crafted and created by God himself, He has given each and every one of us, our very own unique and distinctive (DNA Rhythm! Tempo! Style! Timing And Sound Effects!).

There is another uniqueness called chemistry. The ability to move, flow, work, get along with those in whom you have a connection and kindred spirit. It is a must that you know your God given (R&B) the rhythm and beat of your life, heart, mind, purpose, your destiny, your drive, and potentiality. This should be used for His glory and honor.

From the foundation of the world, you have been equipped with such distinctive chemistry and sound effects that literally moves the very heart of God. Every time you pray, every time you sing, every time you shout Hallelujah! Praise Your Name! Bless You God! Thank You Jesus! It shakes foundations, opens prison doors, and causes walls to fall down flat. This type of praise and sound effect also sets the atmosphere for miracles, signs, and wonders to happen. When God spoke let there be light, the sound effect of the spoken word came into being, and there was light!

Rest assured that you bear a sound unlike anybody else in the world. Yes, at your birth, your mother, father, the doctor, and the Nurses were all waiting to hear your first cry; yes your first cry carried some sound effects, which gave indication, that you were alive and well. Your first cry was not a cry of sorrow. It was the sound of new life and joy.

For anyone in a dark situation and now they can finally see what they could only hear (i.e. like a baby in the womb for the past nine months) should make anybody want to leap for joy. To be in a state of darkness, where you could not see your way out, or see your way through, and now to be on the other side birthed into the light is a good reason to make a joyful noise and throw down some shoe leather at the same time. Give God some relentless praise!!!

Psalm 100 – Is a Hymn of Praise! – **"Make a joyful**

**noise unto the LORD, all ye lands (island, people, nations, You!"**

In the Hebrew tongue it's pronounce **"R-u-wa" "ruwa"** – to make and to create a sudden burst out into a shout of joy, to sound a trumpet or shofar, to cry out with a loud voice, in a war like manner of victory over a conquered enemy! To be noisy, sound an alarm. There are two important Hebrew synonyms **Yowbel** is the joyful sound which is applied to the sound of a trumpet signal (the year of jubilee), **Taqa** is a single blast of a trumpet to summon an assembly. The primary overall meaning of these words is to raise a noise by shouting with an instrument!.

Another Hebrew word for **SHOUT** is **"Shabach"** (Joshua 6) which means to spilt the ears and divide the sound or send the sound in two different directions at the same target. It is the given idea of terrifying your enemy so that it impairs their ability to move. They are attacked without notice because the sound of what they heard confused them and left them disoriented!

I want to enlighten your human and spiritual conscience right about here concerning the biblical definition of shout/shouting vs. dancing. Universally speaking, as baptized believing Christians, we have heard this statement down through generations, "We had a Shouting Good Time" but we meant Dancing." Look back at the definition of shout again, and notice what it says. We shout with our mouth, while we dance with our feet. Here is my point, it wasn't what Joshua and the Children of Israel did in the sixth Chapter. It was what they SAID that caused the walls of Jericho to fall down flat. It's called "SOUND EFFECTS."

These walls were no ordinary walls. The walls were so thick and wide, they would have chariot horse races on top of the city walls. You know the old wise sayings, "The bigger they are, the harder they fall"! (Author unknown)

Psalm 68:1 Let God arise (in and through our shout of Praise) and his enemies will scatter.

Your praise carries that kind of effect. Your Praise –The Hand Clapping, Your Foot Stumping, Your Hand Waving –The Todah and Yadah posture. Your praise has a commanding presence and effect. Psalms 22:3, God inhabits the praises of Israel. He dwells, sits, comes and take up his abode and residence, swells in the midst of praise. Yes, my brothers and sisters according to:

1Peter 2:9 But ye [are] a chosen generation, a royal priesthood, an holy nation, a peculiar people; that ye should show forth the praises of him who hath called you out of darkness into his marvelous light:

Look at the instruction Psalms 100 gives us to follow, adopt, and implement:

Psalm 100:2 Serve the LORD with gladness: come before his presence with singing.

Psalm 100:3 Know ye that the LORD he [is] God: [it is] he [that] hath made us, and not we ourselves; [we are] his people, and the sheep of his pasture.

Psalm 100:4 Enter into his gates with thanksgiving, [and] into his courts with praise: be thankful unto him, [and] bless his name.

Psalm 100:5 For the LORD [is] good; his mercy [is] everlasting; and his truth [endureth] to all generations..

This verse of scripture says it all. For anyone who loves to praise and magnify the name of the LORD, well here it is. Follow His instructions. Enter (i.e. in front of the inner court) with "Thanksgiving" and express your gratitude, by paying homage to offer and give Him praise with the fruit of your lips. Telling the LORD THANK YOU and enter into his courts with praise. In every court of law, we stand when the judge comes in and approaches the bench, as a sign of reverence and respect for the chair/office, and the robe in which he wears to make a ruling either in our favor or against us. Well, God takes on the same posture and position in the midst of our Praise & Worship.

GOD LIVES IN THE PRAISES OF HIS PEOPLE. (i.e. TO CLAP, STOMP, LEAP, DANCE, JUMP, SHOUT, TWIST, TWIRL, etc.) A multiple praise produces a vast amount of multiple miracles!

> Jos 6:5 And it shall come to pass, that when they make a long [blast] with the ram's horn, [and] when ye hear the sound of the trumpet, all the people shall shout (**SHABACH**) with a great shout; and the wall of the city

> Jos 6:20 So the people shouted (**SHABACH**) when [the priests] blew with the trumpets: and it came to pass, when the people heard the sound of the trumpet, and the people shouted with a great shout, that the wall fell down flat, so that the people went up into the city, every man straight before him, and they took the city.

> Psa 98:6 With trumpets and sound of cornet make a joyful noise before the LORD, the King.

> 2Sa 6:11 And the ark of the LORD continued in the house of Obededom the Gittite three months: and the LORD blessed Obededom, and all his household.

> 2Sa 6:12 And it was told king David, saying, The LORD hath blessed the house of Obededom, and all that [pertaineth] unto him, because of the ark of God. So David went and brought up the ark of God from the house of Obededom into the city of David with gladness.

2Sa 6:13  And it was [so], that when they that bare the ark of the LORD had gone six paces, he sacrificed oxen and fatlings.

2Sa 6:14  And David danced before the LORD with all [his] might; and David [was] girded with a linen ephod.

2Sa 6:15  So David and all the house of Israel brought up the ark of the LORD with shouting, and with the sound of the trumpet.

2Sa 6:16 And as the ark of the LORD came into the city of David, Michal Saul's daughter looked through a window, and saw king David leaping and dancing before the LORD; and she despised him in her heart.

2Ch 5:13 It came even to pass, as the trumpeters and singers [were] as one, to make one sound to be heard in praising and thanking the LORD; and when they lifted up [their] voice with the trumpets and cymbals and instruments of musick, and praised the LORD, [saying], For [he is] good; for his mercy [endureth] for ever: that [then] the house was filled with a cloud, [even] the house of the LORD shall fall down flat, and the people shall ascend up every man straight before him.

WE WERE CREATED TO MAKE A JOYFUL NOISE UNTO THE LORD. YES, CALLED TO SET AND TO CREATE A HOLY ATMOSPHERE FOR THE KING OF KINGS, AND THE LORD OF LORD'S. GOD INHABITS THE PRAISE OF HIS PEOPLE!                    **(Revelations 4:11)**

## Look At The Following Examples

ELIJAH BOWED HIS HEAD BETWEEN HIS KNEES AND PRAYED, THEN HE HEARD THE SOUND EFFECTS OF AN

ABUNDANCE OF RAIN HE SAW A CLOUD THE SIZE OF A MAN'S HAND (APOSTLES, PROPHETS, EVANGELISTS, PASTORS, AND TEACHERS)

**(1 Kings 18:28 – 46; Ephesians 4:11)**

THE HOLY GHOST CAME ON THE DAY OF PENTECOST – 50 DAYS AFTER THE PASSOVER AS THE SOUND OF A RUSHING MIGHTY WIND, AND FILLED THE HOUSE WHERE THEY WERE SITTING AND THERE APPEARED UNTO THEM CLOVEN TONGUES OF FIRE. AND IT SAT UPON THEM AND THEY WERE FILLED WITH THE HOLY GHOST AND BEGAN TO SPEAK WITH OTHER TONGUES – PREACHING THE GOSPEL TO THOSE IN THEIR NATIVE TONGUE

**(Acts 2:4)**

SHADRACH, MESHACH, AND ABEDNEGO DID NOT BOW/ BEND/ OR WORSHIP WHEN THEY HEARD THE SOUND EFFECTS OF THE MUSIC

**(Daniel 3: 15-20)**

SOME SOUNDS EFFECTS DON'T OCCUR UNTIL MINIGHT. PAUL AND SILAS PRAYED AND SANG PRAISES...AND THERE WAS A EARTHQUAKE, THAT IT SHOOK THE FOUNDATION, OPENED THE PRISON DOOR, EVERYONES BANDS WERE LOOSED

**(Acts 16:25-27)**

EZEKIEL PROPHESIED TO THE VALLEY FULL OF DRY BONES, AND THERE WAS A NOISE, AND A SHAKING, AND THE BONES CAME TOGETHER! **(Ezekiel 37:1-14) KJV**

O CLAP YOUR HANDS ALL YE PEOPLE - (THIS IS A WORD PICTURE) CLAPPING OF THE HANDS, SUMMONS THE ANGELS OF THE LORD WHICH ARE OUR MINISTERING SPIRITS. SHOUT -"SHABACH" UNTO GOD WITH THE VOICE OF TRIUMPH! **(Psalms 47:1,2; Heb. 1:14) KJV**

GOD RESPONDS TO CERTAIN SOUNDS, "IF MY PEOPLE, WHICH ARE CALLED BY MY NAME, SHALL HUMBLE THEMSELVES AND PRAY SEEK MY FACE, TURN FROM THEIR WICKED WAYS, THEN WILL I HEAR FROM HEAVEN." YES...MAKE A SOUND...CREATE AN ATMOSPHERE FOR SOMETHING TO HAPPEN!
**(2 Chron 7:14) KJV**

GOD INHABITS THE PRAISE OF ISRAEL..SILENCE THE ENEMY...PUT A STROKE ON THE DEVIL! **(Psalm 22:3)**

MAKE A JOYFUL NOISE....IT'S THE PITCH...FREQUENCY THAT EFFECTS THE ATMOSPHERE, STRATOSPHERE, IONOSPHERE, CLIMATE, AND ENVIRONMENT FOR GREAT EXPECTATIONS! **(Psalms 100:1-3)**

IF THESE HOLD THERE PEACE, THE ROCKS WILL CRY OUT **(Luke 19:40)**

SHOUT HALLELUJAH! SHOUT TROUBLES OVER! SHOUT, I'VE BEEN REDEEMED! SHOUT HE SAVED ME! SANCTIFIED ME AND FILLED ME WITH THE HOLY GHOST! I AM GLAD, I'M FREE, I'M HEAVEN BOUND!

I'VE SEEN THE LIGHT FLASHING, I'VE HEARD THE THUNDER ROAR, I'VE FELT SIN BREAKERS DASHING

TRYING TO CONQUER MY SOUL, BUT HE PROMISED
NEVER TO LEAVE ME. NO, NEVER ALONE!

Chapter 8

# The Secret Is Out

**IN THIS SEASON** TELL MY PEOPLE, THAT I AM **REVIS-ITING PROMISES OF OLD!** **WORDS**, **DREAMS** AND **VISIONS** THAT WAS SPOKEN IN SEASONS PAST, AND EVEN DAYS GONE BY, I WILL MAKE GOOD OF EVERY WORD!

**(Numbers 23:19, 20; Isa. 55:10, 11)**

**THEREFORE, SAY TO THE HOUSE OF JUDAH AND TO ALL THOSE THAT WILL HEAR YOU...PREPARE THY-SELF FOR <u>MANIFESTATION</u>...!!!! FOR MY BLESSINGS SHALL COME UPON THEE LIKE A RUSHING MIGHTY WIND - SUDDENLY!**

**(Acts 2:1-4; 1 Cor. 2: 4, 5, 9, 10-16)**

ADMONISH AND ADVISE MY PEOPLE TO BE ON HIGH ALERT, AND IN GREAT EXPECTATIONS. YES, THIS IS THE TIME FOR THEM TO WATCH, SEE, AND HEAR ME WORK AT MY BEST ON THEIR BEHALF.

**(Psalm 62:5)**

I HAVE GIVEN YOU A WORD IN DUE SEASON SAITH THE LORD OF HOST. NOW MEDITATE UPON WHAT I HAVE SPOKEN TO YOU IN SECRET, THROUGH MY WORD, AND HAVE REVEALED UNTO YOU BY MY SPIRIT. NOW GET YOUR MIND, BODY, AND SOULS IN A RECEIVING MODE AND THE BIRTHING POSTURE TO DELIVER!

**(Psalm 102:13)**

SUCCESS BELONGS TO YOU. DONT ALLOW THE ENEMY OF YOUR MIND TO CHEAT AND OR SEDUCE YOU OUT OF MY WORD AND BLESSINGS FOR YOU AND YOUR FMAILY IN THIS SEASON. HAVE I NOT SAID IN DAYS PAST, BELIEVE IN THE LORD YOUR GOD, SO **SHALL** YE

BE **ESTABLISHED**; BELIEVE HIS PROPHETS, SO **SHALL** YE **PROSPER? THEREFORE, I SAY UNTO YOU TODAY, GET READY TO PROSPER LIKE YOU HAVE NEVER PROSPERED BEFORE!!!**

**(2 CHRON. 20:20; JOSHUA 1:8)**

## God's Plan To Prosper You

<u>Gen. 1:26</u> -And God said, Let us make man in our image, after our likeness: and let them have dominion over the fish of the sea, and over the fowl of the air, and over the cattle, and over all the earth, and over every creeping thing that creepeth upon the earth.

<u>Gen. 1: 27</u> - So God created man in his [own] image, in the image of God created he him; male and female created he them.

<u>Gen. 1:28</u> - And God blessed them, and God said unto them, be fruitful, and multiply, and replenish the earth, and subdue it: and have dominion over the fish of the sea, and over the fowl of the air, and over every living thing that moveth upon the earth.

<u>Psa. 8:4</u> - What is man, that thou art mindful of him? And the son of man, that thou visitest him?

<u>Psa. 8:5</u> - For thou hast made him a little lower than the angels, and hast crowned him with glory and honor.

<u>Psa. 8:6</u> - Thou madest him to have dominion over the works of thy hands; thou hast put all [things] under his feet:

<u>Isa. 1:19</u> - If ye be willing and obedient, ye shall eat the good of the land:

Isa. 48:15 - I, [even] I, have spoken; yea, I have called him: I have brought him, and he shall make his way prosperous.

Isa. 48:16 - Come ye near unto me, hear ye this; I have not spoken in secret from the beginning; from the time that it was, there [am] I: and now the Lord GOD, and his Spirit, hath sent me.

Isa. 48:17 - Thus saith the LORD, thy Redeemer, the Holy One of Israel; I [am] the LORD thy God which teacheth thee to profit, which leadeth thee by the way [that] thou shouldest go.

3 John 2 - Beloved, I wish above all things that thou mayest prosper and be in health, even as thy soul prospereth.

## "I Will Give You Power To Get Wealth"

Deut. 8:18 - But thou shalt remember the LORD thy God: for [it is] he that giveth thee power to get wealth, that he may establish his covenant which he sware unto thy fathers, as [it is] this day.

Joshua 1:8 - This book of the law shall not depart out of thy mouth; but thou shalt meditate therein day and night, that thou mayest observe to do according to all that is written therein: for then thou shalt make thy way prosperous, and then thou shalt have good success.

Psa.1:1 - Blessed [is] the man that walketh not in the counsel of the ungodly, nor standeth in the way of sinners, nor sitteth in the seat of the scornful.

Psa.1:2 - But his delight [is] in the law of the LORD; and in his law doth he meditate day and night.

## Keep Your Eyes On The Door
## Something Is About To Happen!

---

### (ACTS 12:5, 13-17)

~YOUR WAITING PERIOD IS OVER~
(I HEAR A PROPHETICAL KNOCKING ON
THE OTHER SIDE OF THE DOOR)
THE DOORS OF YOUR HEART!
THE DOORS OF YOUR MIND!
THE DOORS OF YOUR SPIRIT!
THE DOORS OF YOUR EXPECTATION!
THE DOORS OF YOUR FAITH!
THE DOORS OF THINGS HOPED FOR!
THE DOORS OF YOUR PRAISE & WORSHIP!
EXPECT GREAT AND MIGHTY THINGS TO START
TO MANIFEST!

Job 6:8 Oh that I might have my request; and that God would grant [me] the thing that I long for!

Psa. 21:2 Thou hast given him his heart's desire, and hast not withholden the request of his lips. Selah.

2 Kings 2:9 And it came to pass, when they were gone over, that Elijah said unto Elisha, Ask what I shall do for thee, before I be taken away from thee. And Elisha said, I pray thee, let a double portion of thy spirit be upon me.

Psa. 2:8 Ask of me, and I shall give [thee] the heathen [for] thine inheritance, and the uttermost parts of the earth [for] thy possession.

John 15:16 -Ye have not chosen me, but I have chosen you, and ordained you, that ye should go and bring forth fruit, and [that] your fruit should remain: that whatsoever ye shall ask of the Father in my name, he may give it you.

Matt. 7:7 - Ask, and it shall be given you; seek, and ye shall find; knock, and it shall be opened unto you:

Matt. 7:8 - For every one that asketh receiveth; and he that seeketh findeth; and to him that knocketh it shall be opened.

Matt. 7:9 Or what man is there of you, whom if his son ask bread, will he give him a stone?

Matt. 7:10 - Or if he ask a fish, will he give him a serpent?

Matt. 7:11 - If ye then, being evil, know how to give good gifts unto your children, how much more shall your Father which is in heaven give good things to them that ask him?

Mark 11:22 - And Jesus answering saith unto them, Have faith in God.

Mark 11:23 -For verily I say unto you, That whosoever shall say unto this mountain, Be thou removed, and be thou cast into the sea; and shall not doubt in his heart, but shall believe that those things which he saith shall come to pass; he shall have whatsoever he saith.

Mark 11:24 -Therefore I say unto you, what things soever ye desire, when ye pray, believe that ye receive [them], and ye shall have [them].

Mark 11:25 - And when ye stand praying, forgive, if ye have ought against any: that your Father also which is in heaven may forgive you your trespasses.

Mark 11:26 -But if ye do not forgive, neither will your Father which is in heaven forgive your trespasses.

## AM ABOUT TO SHAKE SOME THINGS UP FOR YOUR BENEFIT!

GET READY TO RECEIVE, AND WALK THROUGH THE DOORS OF MANY GREAT OPPORTUNITIES. "LET THEM

SHOUT FOR JOY, AND BE GLAD, THAT FAVOUR MY RIGHTEOUS CAUSE; YEA LET THEM SAY CONTINUALLY, LET THE LORD BE MAGNIFIED, WHICH HATH PLEASURE IN THE PROSPERITY OF HIS SERVANTS" (**Psalm 35:27**)

IF YOU REFUSE TO PUT ANY LIMITS ON ME SAYS THE LORD I WILL SHOW YOU MANY GREAT AND MIGHTY SIGNS AND WONDERS  (**Psalm 78:41; 84:11; PROV. 10:22**)

"AND SO THAT YOU CAN KNOW AND UNDERSTAND WHAT IS THE IMMEASURABLE, THE UNLIMITED, WITH SURPASSING GREATNESS OF HIS POWER IN AND FOR US WHO BELIEVE, AS DEMONSTRATED IN THE WORK-ING OF HIS MIGHTY STRENGTH" (**Ephesians 1:19 AMP**)

## Note:

*I am aware that this chapter might look a little different from the others but I wanted you to experience God in the same manor that I did when He revealed this Word to me. It's time for the people of God to become aware of the blessings of God and His desire to prosper each and every believer. This is my opportunity to reveal it to you. My prayer for you is that you read over this chapter and each scripture prayerfully in a translation that enlightnes your understanding. If you get a clear revelation from this Word then I have accomplished my goal and I can say with the utmost conviction that The Secret Is Out!*

*Chapter 9*

# It's Not As Bad As It Looks

**Mildred Johnson**
281 Bantry Dr.
Vacaville, CA 95688

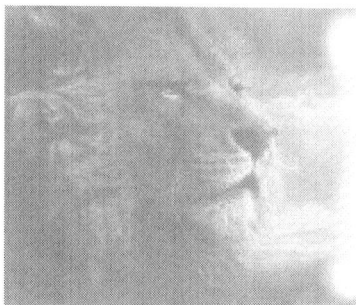

---■---

In the society we live in it is commonly known and said that "image is everything" because of this trend people from every walk of life, are changing their appearance and how they look. Billions of dollars are invested every year into the cosmetic, fashion, and automobile industries to make us feel better about ourselves and how we look to others. (Gen. 50: 15-21; John 11:1-4; Romans 8:28; 1 Pet. 5:10)

### *"Favor is deceitful, and beauty is vain" (Prov. 31:30a)*

Good looks and charisma will get you by, get you through the world's system and accepted into society's status quo but, in the Kingdom of God everything works in the total opposite direction. Good looks and having charisma will take you only where character can keep you. So in the long run what we want to focus on in this chapter is the development of our character and how well we handle the down side, to the up side process, of where God is taking us.

God is big when it comes to productions. God is the master originator when it comes to making block busters. Hollywood and the movie industry show commercials and coming attractions to a theater near you and so does God. God gives you and I dreams and visions, showing and revealing what shall befall us in latter times and what is in our distant future.

Walking by faith is simply trusting, believing and taking God at his word, this also comes along with opportunities of engagements. When believers walk through a series of events it brings them to a process of elimination that brings them to the blessings of the Lord that maketh us rich, and addeth no sorrow with it! For instance:

> Jeremiah 29:11 "For I know the thoughts that I think toward you, saith the LORD, thoughts of peace, and not of evil, to give you an expected end."

Let the record reflect, believers come to know the plans that God has already mapped out from the end to the beginning. (Isa. 46:10) "To Walk by Faith" many times may mean God does not give you all of the details at once, have you noticed that? God is faithful to let you know the final outcome, but very seldom does God let you in on the **"PROCESS."**

God is constantly giving us dreams, visions, and commercials to keep us focused. Yes just a glimpse, here a little, there a little, and then all at once! God works at his best in dark and hopeless situations, especially those special circumstances like in "John chapter 11" where Jesus friend Lazarus had died. Martha and Mary sent word to Jesus and Jesus shows up four days later.

The stench of death and metamorphosis has filled the air. Jesus yet determined that this sickness is not unto death, but for the glory of God, that the Son of God might be glorified. What else is there to think or say? It's not as bad as it looks! "Right?" Right! When things are at there worse, that's the time to become familiar with the Supernatural! Jesus raised Lazarus from the dead with three powerful words of faith, "Lazarus Come Forth"! Martha is converted believes on Jesus Christ, now she's saved, Mary refused to worry therefore she chooses to worship, and once again, the Son of God is glorified, worship is released, and God is exalted!

Eccl. 3:1 gives us to know, *"To every thing there is a season, and a time to every purpose under the heaven."*

We may not want to think that God would use embarrassing times, seasons, and people as part of our journey process in order to prepare us for our destiny. When looking at the life of Joseph, we see a clear picture and gain a better perspective of how God uses all things to work together for our good in the making of a leader and life preserver for Gods family, a people, and a nation. Now let's look at one of my favorite Bible characters found in (Genesis 37) The Life of Joseph.

One of my many favorite scripture readings found in Gen.:37 tells the story of Joseph "A Dreamer of Destiny." At the tender age of seventeen being the eleventh son of his father's old age, (Jacob/Israel) made him a coat of many colors.

Genesis 37:3-11

Now Israel loved Joseph more than all his children, because he [was] the son of his old age: and he made him a coat of [many] colors: 4) And when his brethren saw that their father loved him more than all his brethren, they hated him, and could not speak peaceably unto him: 5) And Joseph dreamed a dream, and he told [it] his brethren: and they hated him yet the more. 6) And he said unto them, Hear, I pray you, this dream which I have dreamed: 7) For, behold, we [were] binding sheaves in the field, and, lo, my sheaf arose, and also stood upright; and, behold, your sheaves stood round about, and made obeisance to my sheaf 8) And his brethren said to him, Shalt thou indeed reign over us? Or shalt thou indeed have dominion over us? And they hated him yet the more for his dreams, and for his words.

9) And he dreamed yet another dream, and told it his brethren, and said, Behold, I have dreamed a dream more; and, behold, the sun and the moon and the eleven stars made obeisance to me. 10) And he told [it] to his father, and to his brethren: and his father rebuked him, and said unto him, what [is] this dream that thou hast dreamed? Shall I and thy mother and thy brethren indeed come to bow down ourselves to thee to the earth? 11) And his brethren envied him; but his father observed the saying.

No matter where Joseph roamed, with this coat of many colors where could he hide? With a coat of this magnitude it wasn't hard to identify Joseph at any time. This no doubt caused friction and a divide in their household, to such a degree, that his brethren could not speak peaceably unto him. Just when you thought things could not get any worse, but all better, the dream begins.

Have you ever been in a similar scenario or know of someone where it seems like God is allowing the envelope to be pushed and pushed. You wonder how much more LORD, when and where does it stop? They hated Joseph because of their father's validation the fact that Joseph was the son of his old age. Ponder on that for a moment. Jacob realized, that he thought it was over for him to be able to have another son at his age.....please cut him some slack even if it's just a little bit!

In all reality, I sense that Joseph is just as shocked as they are, to be on the receiving end of all of these dreams and to know the interpretation is more than a notion. His brothers could not see into the distant future that the dreams and visions were to their benefit as well. Although it was causing and creating a lot of confliction, it was also causing destiny. I trust that you have on your prophetic thinking caps (do you hear the LORD speaking some insight revelation knowledge to you, about where you are and what you are going through right now?)

Joseph was simply telling a dream as a dream. Sometimes believers cannot see that what they are beholding which seems to be uncomfortable at the moment, will in the near future benefit them. So don't fight the process of becoming.

Joseph is left without a choice. He is forced to face the reality of his dreams and the destiny of his life by his brother's jealousy and rejection.

I believe that jealousy and rejection is the launching pad to where you are destined to be all along. If we were to investigate Joseph brother's jealous rage and their rejection, we would find that what they were outraged about had little to do with their younger brother Joseph, and more to do with the timing of his birth. This was by God's divine orchestration and strategy. I have lived long enough to realize that some of the things about you that people might have issues with is more of a God "thang" than it is for you to try and make sense of or take a side and attempt to defend yourself.

Look back over your own life with a fine tooth comb and see what you did not see before. The hell you had to face has more to do with the timing of your arrival here on earth, than you yourself. It has to do with what you bring to the table. It's the effect and affect you walk with. It's in your stride, the way you carry yourself, present yourself, how you see and process life. The bottom line, it's in your DNA! Now how about that? It is the glory of God and the favor He has attached to you. Things just happen when you show up. Yes, "Let the Record Reflect" you don't even understand it yourself, but you know that it is God, through in through, and all in all.

Most people want to zero in on Joseph's coat of many colors, which was a sign of his father's love, adoration, and approval. But in reality, it is way beyond the dyed skin of any animal; The Coat represented a mark that could not be erased, the sign, seal, and assurance of God's every abiding, never ending sovereign grace, and covenant of promise.

Genesis 37:4 – Jealousy, rejection, and hatred the bible admonishes us to note, consider, and believe will move people into a personality conflict where they cannot speak peaceably with you. Right here, you need to know "It's Not as Bad, as it Looks!"

Think it not strange that your birth position (like Joseph) and everything that you have experienced in your Father's House was not for naught. Sibling reviling, the hardship, misunderstandings, seen but not heard, acts of favoritism being shown to some and not all, has been apart of the entire plan, to get you to where you are suppose to be and where you are going to end up when this process is over. "Something good is about to happen for you!"

Now God turns up the heat. It was one thing for Joseph to be born at the close of his father's life then, he is so loved and given the coat of many colors, now comes the all things working together for the good of them who love and are called according to His purpose.

Genesis 37:5 now, here comes the dream. Dreams are God's commercials, advertising, television ads of forth coming events from past predestined futuristic plans. Many times God will give you a glimpse of the future, he will give you without details information pertaining to the how and portions of these things and how they will come to be. He will give you bits and pieces, here a little, there a little, then all at once…are you getting it? We never see the whole thing, until we get to the end, that's when we fully understand the journey process we experienced along the way.

Hard times come to produce strong characteristic traits. Teaching you and me how to hold to a word of promise in the night seasons of our life. Might I encourage you to keep looking back at the dream/visions that you have and the ones you are seeing right now. Things will get better!

Verses 18 and 19 show there is a plot to kill Joseph the dreamer. Keep this in mind people will always attack what they don't understand. His brothers were trying to kill and destroy him, that is the work of the thief.

> John 10:10
> "The thief cometh not but for to steal, kill, and destroy...but I am come that they might have life, and have it more abundantly."

In reality, the closest they could come to touching the dream was to attack the dreamer. Joseph is cast into the pit, sold into slavery and left for dead. Every person of greatness has their day, time, and moment in the "PIT" "Purpose in Transition", "Praise in Triumph and Prophet in Training." Don't allow the appearance of where you are right now rob you of how this platform is about to launch you to where God has destined you to be!

## "You Are Not There Yet"

I've lived long enough to know that all things in life, God used to connect the dots of our life. The dots are defining moments and give definition to the purpose and plan of God for our life.

Remember the words to "Mahogany?" "Do you know where you're going to, do you like the thing that life is showing you, do you know?" I believe that once Joseph got out that pit no doubt, he probably thought that things would start looking better "hmmm" not yet Joe! God had already predetermined that Joseph would be passed from hand to hand in order to situate him for where he was destined to be all along. "A Life Preserver for a Nation" starting with his own family. Friend of mine that's where it all begins, it's with our family.

The people who put you down are simply positioning you to be picked up by someone better and greater. They in turned are now responsible to make sure that you reach the very ones who were responsible for lifting you back up, but higher than you were before.

This is a Kingdom Principle, whenever you are faithful over few, God will make you ruler over many. Don't you love it when you can pass a test? Yes, this enables you to move on to the next assignment and grade. Joseph passed the Pit Test.

What you are going through or what is going through you, trying to flip, toss, or throw you off guard? What is meant by the evil plan and intent of my brothers? Sometimes in life it is the people that we are close too that are the ones that hurt us the most. These are the ones that no doubt will see to it that we make it in life where we are supposed to be and the very ones, who will end up needing us more than life itself.

After the fact that Joseph endured the pit experience, he was elevated to the prison

Therefore, let me encourage you to go through whatever necessary process God has ordained for your development, regardless of what it may look like or even appear to look like. I can tell you from my personal experience, when you get to the other side of where you are right now, you will be ready to go through it or some thing else all over again. Why? Because in the eyes of God, it's really not as bad, as it look!

Keep this some where close by, man always looks on the outward appearance, but God looks at the heart. God is constantly giving us something to look at. Yes God is at his best in dark, hopeless, dead situations, especially those special circumstances that have the appearance and the stench and smell of death written all over it.

Chaos is one of Gods specialties. Have you noticed or even paid attention to the fact that the Lord Jesus is constantly attracted and drawn to those who are the under dogs so to speak. God is drawn to those who are from the other side of the track of life. It really doesn't matter to him. I am amazed at how great this loving wonderful God that we serve is attracted to dark places and the dark side of our lives.

When we look back at the condition and the state of the world in, (Gen.1:2) the earth was without form, darkness (confusion, misery, failure, or defeat) was upon the face of the deep, we also see something else on the horizon and in motion, the Spirit of God hovering they go hand in hand.

No matter how your life may be looking right now, I want to encourage you don't settle for where you are. This is just a temporary holding cell while you are going through this transition. Yes something good is going to come out of this bad, hurtful, embarrassing time and season of your life.

Many times as believers we feel we have to perform or put up this great front as though we have it really going on, when in reality, we don't. If the truth be told the times in which we are fronting the most, are the real times we like many countless others, find ourselves walking through our valley experiences of humiliation (the shadow of death) which on the flip side is God's way and timing of exalting us to higher planes and higher grounds. We don't see let alone understand the path in which God has ordained for us to go. We can always rest assured that after we have been tried in the fire, God will bring forth believers as pure gold.

*Chapter 10*

# NOW

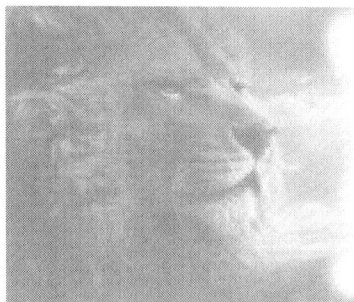

---

I received an invitation from Apostle Layla Caldwell of Tulsa, to come and minister for two days at Agape Outreach International Ministries. My wife, Pastor Shannon and I prayed, fasted and sought the Lord to see which direction the Lord would have me to preach for these two days.

I took a few extra days alone, to quiet myself and my spirit, to hear clearly from the Lord, as to what He would exactly have me share. My Dad, the late Rev. Dr. R.D. Garrison Sr., in his life time always instructed and taught us as young ministers coming up in the ranks, never assume or think that when you have been invited to speak in another Man/Woman of Gods pulpit, that you're going to speak, give, or share some information that they have never heard before, NO...your aim and disposition is come as a voice of confirmation, and information.

Just before leaving home for the airport to catch my flight, I heard the voice of the LORD strong and clear say tell Layla I said "NOW!" Well, as a preaching minister, let the record reflect, there are occasions when we want to come stand before the congregation of people with a prolific, astounding word from the LORD, that will send chill bumps down the spine and want to make your toes curl under.

Well, not this time without a shadow or doubt, I truly had "One Word from the LORD" NOW. God always knows exactly what His people need. He faithfully provides and meets us at the point of our need. No argument out of me, "Father Knows Best!" Once my plane landed and I got to my hotel room and was able to rest up, my routine began.

My day begins with prayer every morning between 3 AM - 6 AM. The Gospel of Matt. 14:25 and Mark 6:48 refers to this time of the morning as "The Fourth Watch of the Night." Jesus is known to be walking, moving, speaking and visiting this time of the morning.

As I begin to pray and ask the LORD for direct, direction and the heart of this one word NOW, here are the foundational scripture references that came to me:

> Psa 102:13 Thou shalt arise, [and] have mercy upon Zion: for the time to favour her, yea, the set time, is come.

> Gen 29:35 And she conceived again, and bare a son: and she said, Now will I praise the LORD: therefore she called his name Judah; and left bearing.

> Hbr 11:1 Now faith is the substance of things hoped for, the evidence of things not seen.

> 1Pe 5:10 But the God of all grace, who hath called us unto his eternal glory by Christ Jesus, after that ye have suffered a while, make you perfect, stablish, strengthen, settle [you].

> Jhn 2:3 And when they wanted wine, the mother of Jesus saith unto him, They have no wine

> Jhn 2:4 Jesus saith unto her, Woman, what have I to do with thee? mine hour is not yet come.

I constantly find it amazingly interesting to watch and see God work through these human clay cracked pots for His glory and honor. It takes the Holy Ghost to connect scripture to scripture and to bring things together. No doubt we would just look at it and not even consider it twice. I am given and driven to know the meaning of words, knowledge is power, right?

So I begin my research on his word "Now" and wow…I am constantly looking, seeking, and pondering various thoughts regardless of the subject matter. Trying to see things from every way possible here's what I discovered through research:

## "Now" Defined

1.) At the present time or this very moment; 2.) Without further delay. 3.) Immediately, all at once: 4.) at the time or moment immediately. 5.) At this very moment. 6.) Not a moment later. 7.) There's no waiting period.

The Lord enabled me though to connect the dots to what He had assigned for me to minister. I want you to envision your life, where you have been and what you have been waiting to happen, materialize, come to pass, come into fruition. Well, when you look at the definition it's not hard to see, that what you have been waiting for is about to show up and show out!

You need to look deeper into your own life and see that, there is about to be no more delays. Yes, there are promises, miracles, unanswered prayers, petitions, hearts desires that are about to be fulfill. Your waiting period just expired! Let's add some biblical text and commentary to what I am saying here.

In Old Testament times whenever the Prophets came to town, the people always wanted to know one thing, "comest thou in peace?" Well, let the record reflect, I went to make an apostolic and prophetic announcement not only to Apostle Layla Caldwell and Agape Outreach International Ministries, but also to that specific region in Tulsa, OK. Gather your thoughts, emotions, and fear and embrace what the LORD is saying right now. It really doesn't matter what hasn't happen up to this point, it's really all about NOW.

When I walked into the sanctuary, praise and worship was going forth, the atmosphere was definitely set and charged for a move of God. While standing in worship, the Holy Spirit spoke to me and said, "Tell my people that the waiting period is over." I thought about the song that (Bishop Walter L. Hawkins wrote back in the 80's era "Don't wait till the Battle is over Shout Now"). If you need some walls to fall down flat, some doors to come open supernaturally, I urge you right now while reading this book and this chapter to lift up your hands open your mouth, move your feet, and just give God all of the praise!

Here what the LORD is saying....it's simple, its one word, Shabach – NOW! Let's look at, and read EZEKIEL 12:21-28

> Eze 12:21 And the word of the LORD came unto me, saying,

> Eze 12:22 Son of man, what [is] that proverb [that] ye have in the land of Israel, saying, The days are prolonged, and every vision faileth?

> Eze 12:23 Tell them therefore, Thus saith the Lord GOD; I will make this proverb to cease, and they shall no more use it as a proverb in Israel; but say unto them, The days are at hand, and the effect of every vision.

> Eze 12:24 For there shall be no more any vain vision nor flattering divination within the house of Israel.

> Eze 12:25 For I [am] the LORD: I will speak, and the word that I shall speak shall come to pass; it shall be no more prolonged: for in your days, O rebellious house, will I say the word, and will perform it, saith the Lord GO.

> Eze 12:26 Again the word of the LORD came to me, saying,

Eze 12:27 Son of man, behold, [they of] the house of Israel say, The vision that he seeth [is] for many days [to come], and he prophesieth of the times [that are] far off.

Eze 12:28 Therefore say unto them, Thus saith the Lord GOD; There shall none of my words be prolonged any more, but the word which I have spoken shall be done, saith the Lord GOD.

You would be wise to agree with what God says and what He sees. Rest assure every word, vision, revelation, promise, prophetic word spoken over and into your life, in past seasons, it's about to happen, materialize, manifest, show up and appear right before your very eyes!

I decree and declare that as you read these words, know that I come into agreement with you, I join my faith with your faith and the threefold anointing that is upon my life as a Prophet, Priest, and King, I declared there shall be no more prolonging of days. I keep sensing and will continue to decree that "Something is About to Happen."

## Daniel 10:10-20
## No More Delays – Spiritual Warfare!

I am inclined to believe that God doesn't waste words. Whenever you read, hear, or received a word from the LORD, you are obligated according to Hebrews 4:1-2 to mix faith within your self and then rise up and go to God by faith and then get ready to receive, be rewarded and expect to be recompensed. Yes, I did say all of that. The day is over for the Body of Christ just barely having average and just enough. We serve the Almighty God, who is Self Sufficient, The Many Breasted One, and The God who is more than enough. I feel a shout coming on, (Hallelujah Jesus)!

I was preaching during our annual Watch Meeting Night 2009 coming into this year of 2010. Nine in scripture is symbolic to completion. The Spirit of the LORD moved upon me to make this decree, command and declaration. "The Principalities will now have to give up, what they have been holding up." This is revelation knowledge!

Don't allow your faith to drop, because of a time delay, waiting with patience on the LORD. Daniel was ministered to and strengthened by the appearance of Jesus Christ. In Daniel chapter 10 verses 5 and 6, three full weeks a total of twenty-one days had past from the first day that Daniel began to pray. From the first day that Daniel prayed, God heard and answered him. The prince of the kingdom of Persia (Verse 13) withstood and held up Gabriel (The Messenger Archangel) with Daniels answer along with the help of Michael, (The Warfaring Archangel).

Know without a shadow or doubt that when you set your face to seek the LORD through fasting, prayer and supplication, while you are calling, God has already answered you!

## Discern The Time And Season That You Are In!

1 Peter 5:10 But the God of all grace, who hath called us unto his eternal glory by Christ Jesus, after that ye have suffered a while, make you perfect, stablish, strengthen, settle [you].

Let me speak to your heart right here, don't be under the cloud of delusion by thinking it is the will of God that you are suppose to go through bad, hard and non-productive times all year, all the time. That is a lie from the very pit of hell. Matt. 4:11 on the forty-first day, one day after Jesus' forty day Fast, the Bible is clear, the devil left him and behold angels came and ministered unto him.

I'm simply telling you recognize when it's your time to be ministered and poured into, revived, refreshed, restored and replenished! God is preparing you for your harvest and reaping time.

> Eccl. 3:1 To every [thing there is] a season, and a time to every purpose under the heaven.

> Eccl. 9:11 I returned, and saw under the sun, that the race [is] not to the swift, nor the battle to the strong, neither yet bread to the wise, nor yet riches to men of understanding, nor yet favour to men of skill; but time and chance happeneth to them all.

You must begin to prepare your mind, heart and soul for a total invasion of 1 Cor. 2:9 – "Eyes have not seen, nor ear heard, neither have enter into the heart, the things that God has in store for those who love and trust him.

God is about to bless you so good, somebody is going to swear that you have done something illegally. Believe me when I tell you that, so much is coming that you won't have room enough to receive it. EL SHADDAI is about to pay you a visit!

### GET IN A STATE OF READINESS!

THROUGH PRAISE AND THANKSGIVING.....WHY DON'T YOU GET STARTED RIGHT NOW, BY THANKING GOD FOR EVERY GOOD AND PERFECT GIFT, EVERY PROVISION, EVERY DOOR THAT HAS BEEN CLOSED – SEE IT OPENED RIGHT NOW, EVERY GRAVE – MUST GIVE BACK THE LIFE IT'S BEEN HOLDING HOSTAGE...EVERY BAD SITUATION – IS TURNING AROUND RIGHT NOW FOR YOUR GOOD!

PRAISE GOD FOR IT NOW - THINK ABOUT IT LATER

LEAH, AFTER SHE HAD CONCEIVED FOR THE FOURTH TIME BEING PREGNANT BY A MAN, WHO WAS TRIFLING, UNFAITHFUL, UNWORTHY, A CHEAT, MANIPULATOR, SCHEMER, DECEIVER, LIAR – DECIDED UNLIKE WITH THE OTHER 3 PREGNANCIES, THIS CHILD IS FOR ME, I'M GOING TO BECOME SELFISH. SHE MADE A DECREE AND A DECLARATION – I HAVE TRIED TO WIN THE AFFECTION OF MY HUSBAND BY GIVING HIM MYSELF AND BEARING HIS SEED, AND REPRODUCING AFTER HIM BUT THIS IS IT…!

THIS IS IT….I'M GOING TO DO SOMETHING I'VE NEVER DONE BEFORE – I'M GOING TO INCORPORATE MYSELF – IT'S TIME TO GO INTO BUSINESS FOR YOURSELF – PROFIT & NON-PROFIT.

SHE SAID IT BEFORE SHE DID IT – STATE YOUR CLAIM TO THE ATMOSPHERE, HEMISPHERE, IONOSPHERE, STRATOSPHERE, CLIMATE, ENVIRONMENT, AND YOUR SURROUNDINGS…

NOW, WILL I PRAISE, BLESS, SHOUT, CLAP, SHABACH - SHOUT, ZAMAR –SING-TEHILAH, KARA-DANCE, REJOICE, TWIST, TWIRL, LEAP, BOW, STOOP, LAMENT, RUN, SKIP——BEFORE——AND——UNTO THE LORD.

> Psa 118:25 Save now, I beseech thee, O LORD: O LORD, I beseech thee, send now prosperity.

> Psa 71:21 Thou shalt increase my greatness, and comfort me on every side.

Now I beseech you to make this an every day practice in your life. Every morning when you wake up make this a declaration and an action. I know sometime you don't feel like it because your situation looks bleak and in your natural vision you can't see your way out. I guarantee you if you make this a routine a daily practice your NOW season will begin right NOW. That's all I have been saying in this entire chapter and book give God the praise and Glory he deserves and he will turn your then into NOW! "Here A Little There A Little, Then All At Once."

## *My Personal Dedication*

I give all Glory, Honor, and High Praise to God my Heavenly Father, for his unsearchable riches and blessings of mercy, grace, and the anointing upon my life, counting me worthy and faithful putting me in the ministry. It is a great honor for me to be able to write my very first book. I have looked forward to this awesome day to be able to write and share my faith, experience, and especially the source from which these writing come, my valued prayer time of Prayer with the LORD, along with my passion for His Presence through Praise & Worship!

I dedicate my very first book to the following people who have touched and blessed my life. I love and appreciate you one and all for all the encouragement you have given and showed to me all of my life. Thank you for adding to the total sum of all that I am, "Here A Little, There A Little, and Now All At Once!

In Honor of my beloved Parents: The late Rev. Dr. Ross Douglas Garrison, Sr., & Mrs. Verdie Lee Dokes-Garrison, I take great pride in dedicating this book to my beloved sainted parents. They taught all ten of their children how to pray, and seek the face of the LORD. Everything that I am and all I hope to be, I owe it to the kind, humble, God fearing parents that you were. I appreciate and love you for leading me to Calvary's Cross and Jesus Christ, My Lord and Savior! Until we meet again!

To My loving and devoted wife, Mrs. Shannon D. Garrison, This project would have been impossible without You! I appreciate the long hours you committed to seeing this project through. As my confidant, best friend, and wife you have always encouraged and covered me in prayer, reminding me of the Word of the Lord over my life, at my low peaks. I am thrilled to see where destiny is about to take us! I love loving you! Your sense of humor and our late night chats, our early Morning Prayer intercession, and most of all "our time of laughter" is what I need and can't live without! Love You Honey-Huna-BOO!

To my Beloved Children: I dedicate this book to you (My 3 Sons) Charles Daniel, Joseph Ross Lamonte, Judah Ross Douglas, (My 3 Darling Daughters) Ashlee Nicole, LaNae Camile, Carla

Henderson. I dedicate this book to you, to your promising future and what God has in store. I can tell you now and up front, it won't all come at once, but it will happen at the appointed time. I encourage you to dream big, take off the limits, this is only the beginning to the monumental greatness that God has in store for our family. The best is yet to come, Love you Dad!

To my Siblings: Verdie B. Jones, Helene - my beloved 2nd mother who reared me. You're forever in my heart ("deceased")! Theresa Harvey, my Brother E.J., Sheila Garrison, Rose Collins (Dave), Pastor Kim L. Garrison (my twin in the Spirit), Charlene Bandy (Clarence) Lottie Mc Coy (Walter). I am blessed and grateful to call you my FAMILY! God has blessed us over the years, and I want you to know that I love you dearly and thank you for the wonderful times we have shared. You are beautiful, warm hearted, caring people to know and be connected to, Love. Lil'D,Aka ("Preacher")

Dad Marshall & Mom Eva (Shannon's parents) Thanks for all your love, support, prayers, and encouragement. I appreciate you our Family Gatherings, the love and the closeness we have shared. Your love is never ending and your encouragement, always on time.

To Judah The Gathering Place Family, one of the greatest Ministries on this planet, I so love, value, honor, and appreciate your love, support, faithful prayers, your commitment, loyalty and undying support. Thank you one and all, we come for standing with Pastor Shannon and I down through these years. Let the Lion of the Tribe of Judah roar!!!

A very special dedication to To Archbishop Mark & Lady Donna Du Bois, Mother Clara Smith, Mom Elizabeth Lane, and To Rev. Dr. Leora Overall, "Chief" Your Prophetic eye and insight has been a consistent guide in my life. I bless the Lord for bringing you into my life. You're a constant City of Refuge and safe haven for me! I appreciate the prophetic impartation and the laying on of hands you have given me so much, and have enriched my life. Your legacy will live on for generations to come. Blessings to each and every one who will read this book and come to discover, that God plans things in stages. Here A Little, There A Little, Then All At Once!

# Acknowledgement

I want to express my heartfelt appreciation first and foremost to Evangelist Sheila Cohen for responding to the prophetic word that was spoken concerning me writing, publishing, and releasing this book, and the many others to follow. The Lord used you to push me into a whole new different arena and atmosphere, which I am grateful and appreciative. I pray many blessings returned upon you, and that the Lord would increase your greatness, and comfort you on every side. I also want to thank your family, your husband Pervis Cohen III and your children for the countless hours you put into this project. Reading, editing, and proofing….Your labor of love shall always stand out as a Monument in my life. Pastor Shannon and I appreciate you from the bottom of our heart, Many Kingdom Blessings be returned to you!

To Prophet Michael Dalton - My Brother Friend, Thank you for writing the Foreword…When the Word of the Lord came out of your mouth concerning the volumes of books that needed to be released, I knew right then and there that you had to be a part of this project. Thank you for your words of grace and prophetic impartation, Blessings!

To Mrs. Regina Bradford Tardy my publicist, you are such a delightsome, warm hearted spirit to know and be around. From the first day you walked into my office, and we began to talk and share our journey and writing experiences, I knew at that very moment, that divine providence was staring us in the face. Thank you for sharing all your wisdom and knowledge with me. I appreciate and regard you in the highest, Thanks Again!

I want to thank my secretary, Ms. Xenia Morris, for helping me to establish the ground work for the business administration, the various ministries and entities that have brought us to the publishing of this project. You are a world of wealth, information, and resources. I appreciate you and your faithful dedication to the Ministry. I pray and bid you Godspeed in all of your endeavors. To my proofing and editing staff, (my sister and daughter) Mrs. Rose Garrison Collins (The Silver Fox), Thanks for being that constant voice pushing and insisting that I begin publishing the chronicles. Well, it's done, and you played a major role in bringing this to pass. This project has brought us closer together as a family. Principal Ms. Carla J. Henderson (my Daughter), Wow, we did it...! Thanks for the "Educator Version" and keeping me on point from the scholastic perspective! The many hours you labored and endured with me, the going back and forth with countless emails, all those adjustment to make sure that everything was in its proper place and saying what needed to be said!

The Testimonial Endorsements: I want to thank and give special recognitions to my fellow colleagues in the Gospel Ministry and friends for their testimonial endorsements on my first book project. I personally appreciate YOU, taking the time out of your busy schedule and sharing your thought with my readers and for being a vital part of this book. I pray and speak The Blessings of the LORD upon you, your families, and that God would increase your territory and that His hand be with you in all that you do!

To My Editing Staff, now let's get back to work, I have some more work for you to do. I've already started on Vol. 2 the next book. Alright Carla, go get our IHOP and Starbucks coffee...LOL.

Many Kingdom Blessings,

† Apostle Dr. Ross D. Garrison Jr,
Author

## Personal Endorsement

---

A Special Endorsement from a Dear Friend of my
Dad and a Mentor to me…

### by †Bishop Frank Pinkard Jr

The late Dr. R. D. Garrison, Sr., Founder & Organizer of the **Good Samaritan Baptist Church of Oakland Inc.** was a good friend of mine. He was spiritually deep and thoroughly dedicated to the ministry of our Lord and Savior Jesus Christ. I am so grateful that his son Apostle Dr. Ross D. Garrison Jr., has carried on the work that his father started in such a profound way, touching and upholding the lives of so many people.

I have reviewed **"HERE A LITTLE, THERE A LITTLE, THEN ALL AT ONCE."** I find it to be profound, inspirational and very spiritually rich. There is that incident in the scriptures when Israel was on the brink of destruction and Jeremiah the prophet, for being outspoken as it relates to the people and how they disregarded God and His intentions for them, was put into a miry pit. Finally out of desperation someone suggested that they would take him out of that pit to inquire about their status in the sight of God. They brought the prophet in, dripping with the contents of the miry pit and asked him is there a word from the Lord? The prophet Jeremiah promptly said "There is."

In these days when people are no longer spiritually conscious, when they are disobedient, when evil is all around us infesting not only our families but our churches, as well as us individually, I believe that the words the Holy Spirit has revealed to Apostle Garrison are what is needed in a time when we are stumbling in darkness and desperately trying to find orderly lives in a disorderly environment.

I thank God for Apostle Garrison and I pray that this inspired work of his will fall into the hands of many people who will find not only help in their struggle, but directions for their lives. That will cause them to know that God is able. If they will be submissive and dedicated to Him through our Lord and Savior Jesus Christ, their lives will take on renewed meaning and they will discover a joy that they have never had before.

Blessings are upon son Ross, and blessings are upon those who are privileged to read his words.

I urge you for your own spiritual betterment to not only prayerfully read, but share **"HERE A LITTLE, THERE A LITTLE, THEN ALL AT ONCE."** Will you please, for someone who you know who is struggling give it as a gift, a copy of this profound word that will glow new light on their pathway.

†*Bishop Frank Pinkard Jr.*
Pastor, Evergreen Baptist Church
Oakland, California

# FINALLY!

And these all, having obtained a good report through faith, received not the promise: God having proved some better things for us, that they without us should not be made perfect. Wherefore seeing we also are compassed about with so great a cloud of witnesses...
Hebrews 11:39-12:1

Finally, God has raised a man after his own heart, which is bold enough, transparent enough, broken enough to tell the real story. What the body needs more than anything in this hour is not another formula, hidden mystery, exegesis, or revelation. The body needs to see the word made flesh and that same word walking among us so that we might touch the humanity of it, and gain courage to believe that we can both do and become the same.

Bishop Ross leads us all the way the Lord brought him through his wilderness experience not just to inherit the promise land, but to discover he is the land himself. We are excited for the pages of your life you have allowed us to read, engrave and behold. We are convinced, this is the Lord's doing. We concur that this is your rainy season, Man of God. Continue to pour and be poured out so that many who are parched and dry can receive a much needed refreshing. We can already hear the sound of the abundance. This much needed supply is not coming out of heaven, but it is the outpouring of the life of true men and women of God. It's beginning to rain!

*Archbishop Mark A. Du Bois*
ABBA International Ministries

\* \* \* \* \*

One of the most difficult tasks we face as believers is understanding "The Process." In this book, Bishop Garrison not only explains the process but he takes us on a spiritual journey of understanding each facet of our walk. He then speaks prophetically to our "Now" and eventually our destiny. What an incredible weapon to have in our spiritual arsenal that is mighty through God pulling down strongholds and casting down every imagination that exalts itself against the knowledge of God.

*Pastor Clinton Foster*
City of Refuge International Church
San Diego, CA

Apostle Dr. Ross D Garrison Jr., has the ability to take you and move you forward bringing fire and passion to your walk of faith. He is the one to bring solid step-by-step guidance, to a life of divine abundance. Words cannot adequately express the tremendous impact that Apostle Garrison has had on my life and ministry. I know this book will strengthen and encourage you and no matter how great the storm, the trial or test, it will move you forward.

His teaching gives you the keys to unlock and transform your thinking into that which says, "Now is the time to decree and declare the word of the Lord!" This is a "must read" book for every man, woman and born again believer.

*Apostle Dr. Joyce E. Scott*,
Founder - New Life Ministries International
Chester, PA

*  *  *  *  *

Grace, Peace, and Blessings! Apostle Garrison, First of all I would like to thank you for allowing me the awesome privilege to read over the excerpts from your book. I must say that it is a tremendous blessing from beginning to end. I would also just like to thank God for using you in this hour to bless this generation with such relevance in this season where people are giving up and don't know which way to turn. Not understanding that God has already declared the end from the beginning. Last but not least I would like to thank you for the word that was released in our house, (NOW) we are eternally grateful to you, and to God for your ministry, just know that our church will never be the same again.

—I Remain, Forever Grateful,

*Apostle Layla Caldwell*
Agape Outreach Ministries
Tulsa, OK

Apostle RD Garrison is the voice of one crying in the desert, make straight way for the Lord. He's definitely a modern-day Apostle/Prophet who has caught the heartbeat of the Father, by modeling his heart, character, integrity and creative ability. Apostle Garrison brings a genuine understanding of the word of God by giving simplistic time bound thoughts that bring a dynamic power and demonstration though the spoken Rhema from the Logos. Apostle Garrison has the true heart for ministry by valuing many diverse relationships that shows the nature of God, though "Here a little, There a little and Then All At Once. I pray many people receive their breakthrough/miracles from this a true-time proven/seasoned Apostle/Prophet , who wasn't just called but elected by God before the foundation of the world to declare /decree his counsel to the nations. So sit back, relax and enjoy this powerful word from the Lord. And it is so!!

***Prophet Fred Brown Jr.***

The Brown family loves you dearly!!

\* \* \* \* \*

After reading ***"HERE A LITTLE, THERE A LITTLE, THEN ALL AT ONCE",*** I felt a sense of clarity regarding my purpose and mandate to the body of Christ. Through this book, I've been challenged to raise the bar and intensity of my prayer life. If your life has been likened unto an unfinished puzzle, this book is a must read. For anyone searching for the answers to the question of their purpose and destiny, this book just makes sense.

***Apostle Anthony Willis, Presiding Prelate***
P.U.R.E. Ministries Int'l Fellowship of Churches

\* \* \* \* \*

Dr. Garrison's Here a little, There a little, Then all at once is a must read for everyone who has a prophetic word over their life. It sums up the power of diligence, submission in the process, and the preparation for "a suddenly" breakthrough. With God, the Alpha is never complete without the Omega…what you're waiting on is finished, but when it manifests depends on you.

***B. Dwayne Hardin, Apostle***
Kingdom Embassy/Millennium Masters, Inc.

Finally! An epistle which speaks not only to leaders, but to the entire body of Christ! Here a Little, There a Little, Then all at once is a prophetic declaration and proper pronouncement of this moment. It is more than just a 'now' word, or a mere slogan but rather discernment of the times articulated in such a way that it is unmistakably the oracle of God in these latter times. Apostle Garrison and this work are as 'one born out of due season' tried in the crucible of God's own making and in the fullness of time has torn away the veil of our current experience, and has drawn back the curtain which has obscured our understanding and brought clarity and revelation. This writing is not an echo of popular post-modern church thought; in contrast, it is Word. A penetrating voice "crying in the wilderness.

Sincerest regards,
† *James D. Adams*

# Reference Information

All scripture reference from the **King James Version** of the Bible
From the engine website of blueletterbible.com.

Word definition source – Hebrew/Greek Strong's Concordance
From the engine website of Blueletterbible.com
Blue Letter Bible
Administered by Sowing Circle Ministry (founder)
Private operating foundation (non profit 501 © (3)
Founded: November 1995
Distributors: Calvary Chapel Magazine
Koinonia House
BIB website

Dictionary.com LLC.
555 12th Street Suite 500
Oakland, California
The American Heritage Dictionary of the English language Third Edition
Copyright 1996, 1992 Houghton Miffin Company
Webster's revised unabridged Dictionary
Published 1913 by C & G Merriam Co.
Copyright 1996, 1998 by MICRA Inc. of Plainfield NJ
Last edit February 3, 1998

Theme from Mahogany "Do you know where you're going to"
Written by: Michael William Messer and Gerry Goffin
Co producer; Carole Bayer Sager
First release 1973 by Artist Thelma Huston
Re-released 1975 by Diana Ross
Motown Label/ founded 1959 by Berry Gordy Jr.
Universal Music Group: Parent label

Walter Hawkins Love Alive III Produced by Walter Hawkins
"When the battle is over"
Composed by Walter Hawkins
Copyright by Leeodd Music/Libris Music (BMI)
1984 Lexicon Music Inc
Light Records

# OTHER MEDIA MINISTRY RESOURCES & PRODUCTS

## SINGLE CD COLLECTION
Advancing Through Adversity
Chosen Praise For A Chosen Generation
A Satanic Desire Cancelled
Opposition and Adversity-The Stage For Manifestation!
Failure Is Not An Option
Restoring The Divine Order of Worship
Policy and Government

## CD & DVD'S COLLECTION
The Kingdom Shift
Established As A Praise In The Earth
Becoming Familiar With The Supernatural
Responsible For His Presence
Living Without Limits
Worship By Design
The Blood That Made The Difference

## OTHER WRITINGS
My Confession of Faith
It Ain't Going Down Like This

Bishop Saylike Productions/Publishing
Judah The Gathering Place
www.judahgathering.org

It is my prayer that reading this book has inspired you to become all that God has created you to be. I would love to hear from you so I can experience your breakthrough along with you.

If you would like to share your comments leave a little note expressing how **"The Judah Apostolic & Prophetic Chronicles...Here A Little, There A Little, and Then All At Once"** has spoken to you, enhanced your life, ministered to you in any way my email and web site information is below and I would love to hear from you.

If you're ever in the Oakland/San Francisco Bay Area and desire a place to worship and experience a move of God through Praise, Worship and the Word, we welcome you to join us at:

**Judah The Gathering Place -**
**8055 Collins Drive Oakland, California 94621**

You can view our live streaming @ www.judahgatheringlive.org on Sunday Mornings @ 11AM and Wednesday Nights at 7:30 PM Pacific Standard Time.

If this book has been a blessing to you,
and you would like to send a prayer request, contact:

**R.D. GARRISON JR MINISTRIES INC.**
P.O. BOX 2206
DUBLIN, CALIFORNIA 94568
Website: www.rdgarrisonjrministries.org
Email address: bishoprdgarrison@aol.com

**Bishop Saylike Productions - Publishing Company**
Email address: saylikepubco@aol.com
Telephone 1-888- (9Saylik) 927-9545

## Bishop Saylike Productions - Publishing Company
Email address: saylikepubco@aol.com
Telephone 1-888- (9Saylik) 927-9545

## ORDER FORM

(PLEASE PRINT ALL INFORMATION)

Name: _____

Address: _____

City: _____ State_____ Zip: _____

Email: _____

Book [  ]  Single CD [  ]  CD & DVD Collection [  ]

Title: _____

Amount Requested: _____  Total: _____

### R.D. GARRISON JR MINISTRIES INC.

*Checks Made Payable to:*
**Bishop Saylike Productions**
P.O. BOX 2206
DUBLIN, CALIFORNIA 94568

Email address: bishoprdgarrison@aol.com
bishopsaylikeproductions.com

visit our website at:
www.rdgarrisonjrministries.org